Food is a Feeling

Food is a Feeling

RECIPES & STORIES, WITH LOVE

Carla Lalli

Photographs by
Lucia Bell-Epstein

Clarkson Potter/Publishers
New York

Dedicated to all cooks, everywhere

Funny thing is, life in that place wasn't like it is here. It took me a few days to realize, but that place went by different rules. There, dogs were in charge. People were animals, and animals were people. You must admit, Dad, the dogs treated us pretty well. They gave us food. They bandaged our wounds after licking them. And they never bit us, even when we tried to hurt them. And every morning they gave us chocolate to eat, because dogs mustn't eat chocolate, you know. Lamb, which is my favorite food, was a rare treat, and the dogs mostly kept that for themselves. For the first few days I refused to eat, and I waited for leftover lamb chop, but someone else always got to it first. So eventually, I just ate the chocolate because there was lots of it around. And I didn't like it much, but it was better than going hungry, so from then on, I ate chocolate every day. And here's the conclusion I came to: It's better to eat something that's always available when you're hungry than to depend on something that runs out early every morning.

—Liz, *Kinds of Kindness* by Yorgos Lanthimos and Efthimis Filippou

Contents

About the Recipes (and Other Stuff)

Hi. ♡

As a cookbook author, former magazine editor, and current food writer, I've been taught that recipe style—the voice, structure, and technical language used to write a recipe—should stay consistent over time. Regardless of where my previously published recipes have appeared or when they were written, I'm supposed to mimic their language when I come up with new ones.

Welp, that's not what's happening here. With due respect to my former self and to anyone who has cooked my dishes before, it didn't feel right that my recipe voice should stay the same, because I am not the same.

I wrote this book during a tumultuous, pensive, painful, joyful, transformative, celebratory, solitary, and exciting time in my life. The precipitating event was the dissolution of my twenty-four-year marriage; while I was experiencing the feelings and phases that followed the separation, I fell completely in love with cooking and eating again, and with myself as a cook. As I moved through that crisis, I became overwhelmed with thankfulness for the role food has played through all my years—as part of my nurturing and upbringing, as an education, as a practice, as a career, and as an outlet. With clarity, I saw the way I cooked as a reflection of who I am.

Food has always been about more than sustenance for me, and it coalesced in a deeper way when I started figuring out who I was going to be as an unmarried person. I took note of the cravings I was having and the meals I wanted to make. I drew on countless memories—muscle and temporal—while I cooked for myself and others. I made favorites. I made new things. I made a lot of popcorn. In many ways and on many days, what I ate was the only good thing that happened. On other days, the cooking was an expression of my happiness or the love I had for the people around me. This experience made me think critically about what comfort food means; it opened me up to the idea of self-care in a noncynical way; and as someone who has been writing about food, feelings, and family for many years, it gave me a new purpose.

Eventually, I decided to write about . . . all of it. As this book took shape, I chose to share personal stories from various phases of my life and my career in food and link them to my meals. The essays and the recipes live together here, on purpose, the way they coexisted in real life.

Because of that, and because of the new perspective I'm bringing to my work as a recipe creator and food writer, the tone of my recipes was destined to change. I think they sound more like me now. If I say to do something a little differently in this book than how I've described it before, it's because there's more than one way to do everything. I don't always dress a salad or season beans the same, and I don't think you have to, either.

I wrote highly specific recipe instructions for many years. Somewhere along the line, I got disconnected from the meaning of the food. It took heartache and a bunch of wild and fantastic transitions that followed to remind me to lean into the internal monologue that plays for me—and I think most of us—when I cook. The memories of being cooked for by others and the way the food makes us feel is what matters. There is no shortage of cookbooks that provide editorial service and no-nonsense instruction, including the two I wrote before this one. For *Food is a Feeling,* I prioritized the emotional service that food and cooking can play in our lives. Less tangible, more elusive, but ultimately more magical.

These recipes sound a little different, but they work. They are written with specificity to guide you when it matters, and suggestively when being loose is the vibe. There are temperatures and times, just as much as there are handfuls and enoughs. I want you to be present for the cooking happening in front of you—what it looks and smells like, what it reminds you of, what's different this time from last time, and when it seems right. I'm not going to tell you that a shallot is a Spin It (my phrasing for an ingredient substitution) for an onion, or fennel for celery, or skin-off chicken instead of skin-on. I'm starting to think you don't need me for that. If the bowl needs scraping, scrape it. If the sauce needs salting, salt it. If there are more people, double it. If it's just for you, eyeball it. If it's what you like, make it. If you'd do it a different way, change it.

Cooking is creating. It is, by nature, transformative. I'm here for you as a mentor and a guide—always—and I believe in your unique skill more than ever. As much as I'm honored to be part of what happens in your kitchen, you're the cook in your home, not me. I hope this book finds its way to your bedside table or on the floor next to where you drop your pillows before turning off the light. I hope it ends up in the kitchen, too, and I want you to rest your messy spoon on the open pages.

This is how I see you: in your burrow, the lights on and candles lit, surrounded by the music you like or the voices of the people you adore, doing your thing. I trust you implicitly to make great food, but also to make it mean something to you. With confidence and freedom, I bequeath you the longest rein.

Love always,
Carla

Buttered Rice

The first night I spent in the sublet apartment, separate from my children, separated from my husband and home of twenty-four years, I cooked and my sister came over.

My sister, Nina, had to wear me down to have her over, so reluctant was I to be the reason she had to leave her small children and drag ass to this stranger's apartment. *I'm fine, I'll be fine, I like being alone, you don't have to come.* Nina persisted. Finally, I admitted, *Yes, I would like you to be here and, no, I don't think I should be by myself.*

The sublet, on the second floor of a carriage house in Brooklyn, was all wood beams and exposed brick with two big skylights. It was where my ex and I would stay, alone, on alternate weeks while we figured out our new lives. Whoever wasn't at the apartment would be back at the house with our two children. It was a lo-fi, hand-built place with wide plank floors through which light and pot smoke rose from the artist's studio below. There was a wall of books and happy houseplants in pots on every windowsill and in every corner. The living room was outfitted with a thin-cushioned blue velvet couch, a sheepskin rug, and a wood-burning stove. I don't think there was a lightbulb in the place over 40 watts. The owners had installed a giant crystal into a central skylight, which leaked when it rained; more crystals hung from the ceiling and projected rainbows on various walls all day. The open shelves in the kitchen were stocked exclusively with clear glass jars housing healthful pantry items: lentils, beans, every variety of rice, multiple types of flour and honey, Himalayan pink salt, and decanted pasta shapes. If Winnie the Pooh left the forest to become a naturopath, this would be his apartment.

I met my husband when I was twenty-three, got married when I was twenty-six, and was happy in my marriage for more years than I was not. But our average had plummeted: too many lows in a row. For several years, I had made a lot of pragmatic choices I hoped would make our relationship better: If I was unhappy, I should work on that. I found the right therapist and showed up every week. I accepted my brain's delightful chemical mix of depression and anxiety and got treatment for both. I stopped smoking weed. I tried to be a better parent. I started lifting heavy weights and the back pain I'd carried around for almost two decades went away. I wrote two cookbooks that did very well, and I became a video host.

Life got better, but the marriage stayed stuck. The decision to separate was ultimately mutual, but for a long time I carried guilt about putting my happiness first.

Despite months of processing in solo therapy and in couples therapy, my preparations for the first night away were not thought out—at all. On that surreal day in mid-May, I brought my rolling suitcase up to the laundry area on the top floor of our family home and surveyed the heap of clean clothes piled there. I chose belongings at random and dropped them straight into the bag at my feet. Then I prowled back and forth between the bathroom and the bedroom, foraging: I needed my meds, mouth tape, the journal I rarely wrote in, and quite a few lip glosses, apparently. Phone charger, computer charger, sunglasses, Advil. There was no tearful, cinematic moment when I removed my wedding ring and put it into a jewelry box. I had stopped wearing it months before.

Personal items secured, I went down to the kitchen. If I were going on a plane trip, I'd prep my own snacks. For this one-of-a-kind voyage, I filled a tote with random kitchen items:

· a bunch of Tuscan kale from the veggie drawer;

· one head of garlic;

· an opened bottle of everything bagel spice;

· a jar of red pepper flakes;

· the extra peppermill we kept on the dining table;

· half a stick of butter;

· an opened bag of white rice;

· popcorn kernels;

· a bottle of olive oil;

· half a pound of dried beans;

· and a box of loose black tea.

I don't know if this is an objectively sad assortment of things, or if it just would have made me sad for my children to see my choices. None of that matters, though, because the only other heartbeat in the house that afternoon belonged to Peg, my cat, who I said good-bye to. Then a quick, surreal drive over to my new digs. When I got to the top of the single flight of stairs with bags hooked on my shoulders, elbows, and in my fists, it hit me that the moment I'd been visualizing for months was real.

One of many buttery rice leftovers

The kitchen at the sublet

I unlocked the door, swung it open, and took a picture of what the apartment looked like from where I stood on the threshold. You know, for later. Sunshine was streaming through the skylights, illuminating the four-burner stove set into an L-shaped thick wooden counter on the far side of the room. (I didn't know it then, but the idea for this book would come to me after a meal I cooked in that hippie kitchen.) With one foot in my life as a newly single person, I felt relief. I felt content. It was too soon to miss my children. I felt my lungs open. I stepped inside, put my stuff down, and took a bare-faced, smiling selfie that I sent to a close friend. I unpacked.

A few hours later, it was dark out, and Nina was on the way. While I waited, I cooked. I had the garlic, the oil, the butter, the half bag of rice, and the kale. The butter had gotten squished by the other groceries, but was salvageable. I took out the apartment owner's Dutch oven, red, six quarts, which was way too big for the amount of rice I had, but I was going to make it work. I cook a lot of rice, and 99 percent of the time, I steam it, either in my rice cooker or on the stovetop. That night, though, I started with fat. Maybe the softened stick of butter was calling to me. Or the proportions of the pot made bringing a cup and a half of plain water to a boil feel skimpy. Or maybe everything else I had to cook was too austere; no flesh, no fish.

I used a wooden spoon to scoot a few tablespoons of butter off the waxy wrapping paper and into the warmed-up pot. I watched it melt and then foam. I added the rice. I stirred, coating the rice with butter, listening for the glassy sound the grains make when they start to heat up. I seasoned the rice with salt and poured in the water, which sizzled. I covered the pot and set a timer for 18 minutes, a duration for rice cooking imprinted on my being.

Rice in motion, I stripped the leaves off the kale and tore them in half. I squeezed a few garlic cloves in my pincers, stem against my thumb, bending them to loosen their skins, a trick I'd learned recently. I teased off the skins. I set a cast-iron skillet over medium-high and acknowledged that the apartment was equipped with exactly the bare minimum of quality equipment that would allow me to make pretty much anything. Nothing flashy; no stainless; no nonstick. Three cast-iron skillets hung from fat nails set into a vertical wooden beam next to the stove: one just big enough for a couple of eggs, one large enough for a pork shoulder, and one perfect for tortillas. On a shelf beneath the counter, there was a covered saucepan, an enameled butter warmer, a couple of colanders, a glass lasagna pan, and an electric tea kettle. Beneath that, a huge stockpot. It wasn't my 25-year accumulation of kitchen equipment, yet nothing was missing.

I poured a generous amount of olive oil into the skillet, as I always do, then added the garlic. I seasoned it with salt and pepper before adding the kale, and seasoned that with salt and a big pinch of the red pepper flakes I'd brought with me from home.

When the rice was ready, I scooped it into two small bowls and put the kale on top. The first thing my sister said when she tasted the rice was:

Mmmmm, did you cook this rice in butter? So good.

I haven't cooked rice in butter in literally years, I told her, explaining that I'd measured nothing and made it in the wrong-size pot but used butter, and it was the most perfect pot of rice I have ever made. *It's actually annoying.*

Mom always cooks the rice in butter, she said.

Always.

The butter makes it so good.

I know, I said, *her rice is always so good. She doesn't even rinse it!*

And then: *Frank loves rice so much.* Frank is our father.

I love rice so much, she said.

I love rice, I said.

We ate our buttered rice and our kale and drank beer. We talked about how weird this night was. Nina was nineteen when I got married; we've barely ever experienced single-older-sister-solo-apartment times. An irrational giddiness came over me. It was coming from feeling—for the first time in many years—unburdened. I was no longer coming to terms with the hardest decision of my life. It was happening.

After Nina left and I went to bed, I relished how it felt to sleep alone, without my back turned to anyone.

I wasn't cooking for my sons or my husband that night. I was cooking for my comfort. Unconsciously, I cooked like my mom. There were no technical flairs, and to be honest the portions were kind of small. Dinner seemed improvised with what I threw into my I'm-going bag. Sort of. The truth was that I started composing that meal as I packed. Everything Nina and I ended up eating had a direct line back to my upbringing and the food that my mom made for me, for us, which is why I packed those ingredients. The kale that was in countless Sunday soups; the garlic rubbed raw onto fried bread or melted into spaghetti with clams every week; a three-liter can of olive oil in the pantry, always on backup; the covered pot of buttery rice I'd sneak spoonfuls out of before dinner.

I didn't yet know what to do or who to be without my family. I was keeping busy doing the thing I always do: figuring out what was in the house and deciding what I could make, pulling out a pot, and cooking. The day was fucked on so many levels, and I was wholly unprepared for the deeper lows in my immediate future. I also had no inkling of the happiness that would hit after the roughest bit was over. Everything in my life was about to change; food was going to be the constant that kept me together. Later, with perspective, I'd see how cooking was an emotional survival skill that I could leverage on sad days, on joyous days, and all the days in between.

When you're cooking, you get to just cook. Making something to eat gave me the ability to empty out my brain and indulge in predictable pleasures: the sweet smell of butter in the pan, the green-gray tinge on my thumb pad from stripping kale off the stem. Nudging garlic around in hot oil with someone else's wooden spoon. The curative properties of fire, time, heat, iron, wood, skill, smoke, and a little magic.

Face on arrival

Greens, Garlic, and Mom Rice
For 2

3 tablespoons butter

1 cup white rice (any type), rinsed and drained well

4 garlic cloves

1 bunch kale (any type)

Extra-virgin olive oil, for drizzling

Kosher salt; freshly ground pepper

Crushed red pepper flakes, for seasoning

In a 1½- or 2-quart pot with a lid, melt the butter over medium heat until it foams. Add the rice, season it, and cook, stirring, until the rice is buttered up and shiny and starts to make a glassy sound against the surface of the pot, 2 to 3 minutes, max. Pour in 1¼ cups water (or chicken stock, or water and a bouillon cube) and bring to a simmer. Cover the pot, set over the lowest heat, and cook (without peeking or stirring) until the rice is tender and the liquid has been absorbed. This takes 18 minutes. In a thin-walled pot, it will go faster. If your low is super low, it might be longer. Turn off the heat, fluff the rice, then keep it covered.

While the rice cooks, peel the garlic and smash it to bits, or slice it. Strip the kale off the stems and tear the leaves into big pieces. Or small pieces. Heat a skillet over medium, then add a generous drizzle-drazzle of oil to the pan. Add the garlic and cook, stirring and turning occasionally, until light golden. Add the kale and toss to coat with oil. Season with salt and black pepper and a pinch of red pepper flakes. Cook until the greens are tender. If the pan seems dry but the kale is not ready, add some water to move it along.

Serve the rice topped with the kale, obviously.

1. Scaling Down

13
14
16
W 24
JUN
Diamond memo

TK amt
potato starch noodle
hot water 10 + 6
2 Tb
unsalted butter
ic cloves smashed
llions / ¼" white
thin greens
sauce
sauce – start w/
n
gar
d sprouts
garlic or chili cris
ve oil
Chil
gs, beaten to blend
heat
garlic, stir + break
ok till golden
r + cover if needed
ven more
/ v dark + v light
ht flavor
starchy center
no crisp
set the dros
recipe order
WFP
mimic kitchen
sles

Upsides to Downsizing Dinner

There are two types of people. The ones who say *Congratulations!* when you tell them you're getting divorced, and the ones who grab your arm and gasp, *That's so sad!*

An actual heart-shaped chicken cutlet

Sure, at the beginning, it *was* odd to cook for three, or two, or one and not our nuclear family of four. I wouldn't say it was sad, though. It was weird. It was unfamiliar. It was quieter.

Once my ex and I had established that I was going to be the one staying in the family home, I thought a lot about what the new regime was like from my younger son Cosmo's point of view. Dad's at his place, brother is at college, and now you get to have dinner alone with your *mother.* From my side of the table, I was still adjusting to not seeing him during my off weeks, and I tried hard not to firehose 100 percent of my attention on him when we were reunited. *Be chill, Mom.* Normalcy is not being grilled for updates every time you see your parent. Even with that restraint on my part, we didn't struggle to find conversation during dinner. Some seats around the table were empty, and that meant he was no longer witness to tension between his parents; he was not trying to find a way in edgewise with his older brother; and I still cooked the whole pound of pasta. This scenario was no one's first choice. But—could be worse.

From then on, the more one-on-one time we spent together, the more our relationship grew. Because our gang-of-two scenario had never really existed before, there were no built-in triggers, and we got to invent a new dynamic as we went.

Cooking for mother and child was objectively easier and less expensive. Cooking a smaller volume of ingredients also took less time. Additionally, what I sold as "dinner" got a lot looser. Hard-boiled eggs and toast with some salami and a big salad? That's a meal. The voices telling me this should be a horrible period quieted as I got into a groove and realized how freeing it was to throw something together on the fly, rather than panicking at 4 p.m. because I didn't have enough protein in the house.

I had a boss who used to say: *There are no problems, only challenges.* He used this to deter complaining, and I thought he'd be pleased to know it also worked as motivation for our evening meals. I was willing to set up a three-step dredging station to make breaded chicken cutlets on a weeknight. There were fewer breasts to flatten, not as many bread crumbs in the mix, and getting everything through the conveyor belt was faster. To cutlet midweek is a treat: Cutlets are the best.

One afternoon I picked up a vacuum-sealed rack of lamb chops for the two of us. High price per pound, yet not as many pounds. Eating lamb always feels special, and I wanted all of my time with Cosmo to be special. We no longer waited for a reason to light candles. It became a part of basic table-setting along with forks and knives, and we played with the wax that flooded the wick and ran down the sides when we were done eating. I loved doing that as a child, and I loved doing it with my child.

Other rituals emerged. A one-and-done pesto pasta became our Monday night special, which then turned into TV dinner night—unheard of as a foursome, but sweet as a couple. We'd sit hip to hip on the floor of the TV room with our bowls on the coffee table in front of us. We like *Bob's Burgers, The Office, Parks and Recreation.* We discovered Cosmo had outgrown his aversion to fish sauce after I added it to a marinade for beef; the resulting stir-fry becomes another weekly staple. Instead of dessert, we closed out our meals with a round of good-faith negotiation: *Are you in the mood to make a deal?* The terms are always the same: How will we divvy up the dishes, who's It for the last dog walk, and who bundles the cardboard recycling. This is *our* thing. It is self-referential only in our unit; it deepens and changes based on the flair one of us brings to the after-dinner wheeling-and-dealing. (For the record, I'd rather load the dishwasher than do yet another dog walk.)

So, no. It's not sad. It's just different.

Sometimes we have stand-up dinner at the kitchen island: steamed (frozen) dumplings and edamame dressed with sesame oil and black pepper; multiple rounds of quesadillas; Mexican delivery from our neighborhood spot. Sometimes, Cosmo comes home late and cooks for himself. I want to observe, but force myself not to hover—mostly because I can't watch the mess unfold. He emerges with steaming ramen that he eats straight out of the saucepot, perfectly fried eggs that he photographs and texts to his buddies, exquisite grilled cheese sandwiches with lacquered surfaces that he parades under my nose. *The trick is mayonnaise and low heat,* he tells me when I beg for a mouse bite.

Big change is uncomfortable, therapy speak I repeated to myself during that transitional time. Cosmo and I talk about what's been hard for him about having to move back and forth between two households, how annoying it is to repeat information for each parent, the awkwardness of those first holidays and vacations we spent without each other. These are the immutable and unavoidable downsides that come with divorce. I have no control over how he'll feel about these changes; I can only try to show up for him when we talk. What's on the table between us, though—for that we both have a say and a shared objective, and one way or another, we know how to get fed.

Always brown the bone side, too

Heart-Shaped Chicken Cutlets
2 servings, when one serving is for a hungry teenager

½ cup cornstarch

¾ cup buttermilk

2 cups panko bread crumbs

Kosher salt; freshly ground pepper

2 boneless, skinless chicken breasts (about 1½ pounds total)

2 teaspoons chili powder

Vegetable oil, for frying

Flaky salt, for serving

Kimchi, Sriracha, Kewpie, and/or spicy mayo (from Lobster Max's Way, page 128), for serving

Place the cornstarch, buttermilk, and panko in three separate dinner plates, pie plates, or rimmed baking sheets. Season each with salt and pepper. If your buttermilk is thick, thin it out with a little water. Line a baking sheet with paper towels.

Place the chicken breasts on a cutting board. Butterfly each breast by slicing it in half horizontally with your knife held parallel to the cutting board; don't cut all the way through. Open the cutlet like a book, with the intact edge as a hinge. The rounded top and narrow bottom of the cutlet will resemble a heart; some imagination may be required.

One at a time, place the cutlets between two sheets of plastic wrap or waxed paper. Use a meat mallet, rolling pin, or the heel of your hand to flatten the chicken to about ¼ inch thick. Season both sides with salt and pepper, then with chili powder, dividing evenly.

Working with one cutlet at a time, press it into the cornstarch, coating evenly, then pat off excess. Dip into the buttermilk, letting excess drip back into the plate. Place in the panko and press to adhere on both sides. Place the cutlets on a second rimmed baking sheet.

Pour ¼ inch of oil into a large heavy skillet (I like to use cast-iron); potentially 1 cup, or more. Heat over medium-high until very hot, 5 to 6 minutes; test readiness with a pinch of breading, which should bubble vigorously on contact.

Cook the cutlets, gently shaking the pan back and forth and rotating it occasionally, and gently lifting them up from one end if needed to let the oil run underneath, until the underside is very dark golden brown and crisp, 3 to 4 minutes. Turn and cook until similarly browned on the second side, about 2 minutes more. Transfer the cutlets to the paper towel–lined baking sheet and season with flaky salt.

Serve the cutlets with kimchi, Sriracha, Kewpie, and/or spicy mayo, as you wish.

Surf and Turf, Except the Surf Is Just from Fish Sauce

Serves 2 to 4

1 tablespoon plus 1 teaspoon fish sauce, divided

3 tablespoons mirin, divided

Soy sauce, for seasoning

Toasted sesame oil, for drizzling

1 pound chuck roast

2 tablespoons fresh lime juice

1½ teaspoons sugar

2 garlic cloves

Thumb-size piece fresh ginger

2 dried Thai red chiles

1 tablespoon peanut or other neutral oil

Kosher salt

Toasted sesame seeds, for topping

Steamed rice and individual lettuce leaves, for serving

In a medium bowl, combine 1 tablespoon fish sauce and 2 tablespoons mirin. Season with a few dashes of soy sauce and a drizzle of sesame oil. Slice the beef against the grain into ¼-inch-thick slices and add it to the marinade; turn to coat. Let sit for 1 hour (or cover and refrigerate overnight).

In a small bowl, stir together 3 tablespoons water, the lime juice, the remaining tablespoon mirin, the remaining teaspoon fish sauce, and the sugar. Finely grate the garlic and about 1 teaspoon of ginger into the mixture. Crumble the chiles and drop them into the bowl, then stir to dissolve sugar. Add a drizzle of sesame oil; taste and adjust seasonings (spiciness will build as it sits).

Heat a medium cast-iron skillet over medium-high until very hot, 2 to 3 minutes. Pour in the peanut oil. Arrange the marinated beef in a single layer and cook until very caramelized and threatening to char on the underside, about 3 minutes (the sugars in the mirin and fish sauce take on color quickly).

Turn each piece and cook briefly to kiss it on a second side; the beef should still be juicy and mid-rare. Season with salt and top generously with sesame seeds.

Transfer the beef to a serving dish and serve with dipping sauce, rice, and lettuce leaves alongside.

Weeknight Lamb Chop Special
For any number

An amount of extra-virgin olive oil, and then more

Kosher salt

Spices or a spice mix (see below)

2 or 3 loin lamb chops per person

Lemon wedges or vinegar, and flaky salt, for serving

Take out a vessel that can comfortably accommodate however many lamb chops you're making. Pour in what you estimate to be an amount of olive oil that will coat them. Add a large pinch of salt for each chop, then season the oil with some spices. Could be cracked fennel seeds and a few pinches of crushed red pepper flakes. Chinese five-spice is nice. A chile-cumin blend. Turmeric and black pepper. Garam masala. These are all very tasty with lamb. If you're not sure, salt and pepper is classic. Coat the chops in the seasonings and oil. If you feel like you did not allow for enough oil or spices after you dress the chops, add more. Let the chops marinate for an hour or two at room temperature, or cover and chill for up to 2 days.

Heat a cast-iron skillet that the chops will fit in snugly without touching. Heat it over medium-high for at least 3 minutes. Add a drizzle of olive oil to the hot pan, then place the chops in on a flat side and lower the heat to medium. Press firmly on the chops to get their cut sides, surfaces talking to the surface of the pan. The bone in the chop is going to get in the way of that contact as the meat shrinks back, so you want to make sure to get some color on them from the jump. As they cook, fat will render into the pan, filling in the gaps between the skillet and the protein and carrying heat, which is essential. Also, lamb fat is the best; don't pour it off.

Cook the chops, turning them from one side to the other and standing them on the fatty edge every couple of minutes, until the chops are truly exquisitely browned on both sides and the internal temperature is around 130°F for pink medium-rare meat, about 8 minutes total, depending on the thickness of the chops. Rare lamb is a little chewy for me, and overcooked lamb can be tough, but cook to your desired doneness.

Let the chops rest at least 5 minutes before cutting the meat away from the bone, and then slicing against the grain. Serve with a squeeze of lemon or splash of vinegar, a drizzle of juices that collect from resting, a little more olive oil, and flaky salt. Include the bone, for nibbling, of course.

The Family Meeting Menu

There are a lot of pragmatic, logistical details to take care of when you get separated after two dozen years of marriage. Finding a temporary apartment, hiring lawyers, pretending you're going to miss the dog.

The last thing left on the list, and the one thing neither of us wanted to do, was break it to the kids. Eventually, we decided when and how to tell them, and agreed on what we'd leave unspoken. But, it was my job alone to figure out what to make for dinner afterward.

I was distracted, anxious, and worried the day my then-husband and I had picked for the Big Talk. It was unnerving to know that our children were clueless about the really rotten news they were about to get, and I didn't like being in control of when that bubble of innocence would burst. It seemed especially cruel to do it over dinner, interrupting a meal in progress with information that could make their stomachs clench. Instead, my ex and I decided we'd have the conversation first, and eat dinner after.

There was dread in my heart as I walked to the market around 3 p.m. that day. I've planned a lot of dinners and designed a lot of menus, but this one had me stumped. What's the right thing to serve for a family fissure? What would my children crave right after I unleashed a mudslide into their existence? The family meeting had started to feel like the closed basement door in a scary movie—I didn't want to go in, and yet there I was, walking straight toward it. Simultaneously, the clock was ticking down to a transitional moment that I was ready for. I'd been hiding my marital unhappiness from my children for years, and that was about to end—ostensibly a positive thing—but only for me. I didn't know how much anger, sadness, and confusion I'd have to navigate on their part.

No, really: What was for dinner? Takeout had sadness written all over it. I was definitely going to cook. Do I double down and make something no one likes, thereby cementing the bummer of it all? "There were lima beans for dinner and I hate lima beans," to quote *Alexander and the Terrible, Horrible, No Good, Very Bad Day*. Or, do I go with something everyone loves and hope that it provides a momentary escape? If that backfired, though, I could ruin a favorite food forever.

A batch of nooch vinaigrette

Standing at the butcher's counter, weighing my options, I went with a classic: pork chops. We ate pork chops once a week throughout the pandemic, and it had a proven track record of providing enjoyment in those dark times. Also now? The chops were meaty, marbled, and fatty; I chose three of them for the four of us. I picked up some sugar snap peas, too. It was spring, after all.

The talk went better and worse than I anticipated. There was heartbreak and shock, some anger, but also an expression of understanding from my younger son that made me realize he wasn't a little kid anymore. When no one had anything else to say, I went into the kitchen to make dinner. I didn't know how to feel, but I knew how to make pork chops, so I did that. Taking down my biggest skillet and clicking on the gas to preheat it, unwrapping the chops to season them, and slicing the peas in half on a pretty bias—it gave the night an illusion of normalcy. Whether I found an escape in what I was doing, or an outlet for my own feelings, or a cover for the levity that was creeping to the surface, I can't say for sure. I had a job to do and I was locked in.

I cooked the pork chops until they were caramelized on both sides and the outer edge of the loin—where the good fat is—was browned. While they rested, I spooned leftover white rice into the same skillet and let it get toasty in the pork renderings. I seasoned the rice with black vinegar and tilted in the juices that had accumulated on the tray the chops rested on. I had made a nutritional yeast vinaigrette that afternoon, which was so good I couldn't stop tasting it by the spoonful, a savory emulsion of vinegar, tamari, garlic, and mysterious nooch in blissful harmony. I used that to dress the raw peas. There was a perfect avocado on the counter—kismet—which I quartered and tucked onto the edge of the serving plate with the rice. I cut the chops off the bones, then sliced the meat into thick strips, which makes it easier to share. My older son declined to join when called to the table, but the rest of us ate. Quietly, which seemed right, given the circumstances.

Later, a little surly and not at all chatty, my firstborn came down and made himself a bowl of rice topped with meat and took it to the TV room, which is normally not allowed. I was happy he was eating, though. His willingness to partake (on his own terms) signaled to me, perhaps wishfully, that somehow everything was going to be okay. No one flipped the table over, no one stormed out. We all went to bed under one roof—sad, but not hungry.

Segueing from the separation conversation to pan-frying pork chops felt surreal in the moment. To not cook would have been truly bizarre. Crap things were happening, but omitting dinner would have only made it worse. That's what I thought, or hoped, or hoped might be true, providing a convenient justification for my actions. Maybe it could simply be what it was: a family meal that I cared about making well, and wanted my family to enjoy. Did it matter that this meal wasn't horrible on an otherwise shitty day?

My eldest was home between semesters from college a few weeks ago, and I made pork chops, with rice (surprise), and a big salad dressed with nooch vinaigrette, which is almost always in the fridge, even after all this time. When he came to the table he said, *Ooo, pork chops, classic.* If anyone was thinking it, no one mentioned the night of the rotten family announcement. I sat at the head of the table, flanked by my boys. We put chili crisp on our chops and my younger son packed up what was left over for his lunch the next day. Sometimes, miraculously, a pork chop can just be dinner.

NOOCH

Nutritional Yeast Vinaigrette
Makes 4 cups

Adapted from Griffin Wilson and Handline restaurant

1½ cups nutritional yeast

⅔ cup tamari, liquid aminos, or soy sauce

¾ cup apple cider vinegar

4 tablespoons minced garlic (about 6 large cloves)

2 cups grapeseed or other neutral vegetable oil

In a blender, food processor, or hand blender jar, combine the nutritional yeast, tamari, vinegar, and garlic and blend to combine. With the motor running, slowly drizzle in a few tablespoons of oil until the mixture looks creamy and emulsified. At this point, you can pour in the remaining oil a little faster; use all of it. The dressing will be thick, glossy, and homogeneous. If it's too thick for your liking, thin it with a little bit of water. Taste and adjust seasoning with additional tamari and/or vinegar, as desired.

A quart of dressing may seem extreme, and you can certainly halve the amounts if you prefer. But once you have it in the house, you will find many excuses to consume this daily. It's amazing on any salad greens but also makes a ridiculously delicious dip for crudité, a perfect little sauce for roasted chicken or grilled fish, and it can be used as a sandwich schmear.

Get ahead: Cover and refrigerate dressing for up to 10 days.

Separation Pork Chops
4 servings

4 pork rib chops, 1 to 1½ inches thick (about 3 pounds total)

Kosher salt; freshly ground pepper

Extra-virgin olive oil or vegetable oil

4 cups leftover (cold) cooked rice or grains, or freshly cooked rice

Black vinegar or sherry vinegar, for seasoning rice

1 lemon, cut into wedges

Flaky salt and chili crisp or hot sauce, for serving

Choose a cast-iron skillet big enough to accommodate the chops, or two skillets big enough to hold 2 each, or work in batches. Place the skillet or skillets over medium and heat for 3 to 5 minutes minimum.

Pat the chops dry, then season on both sides with salt and pepper. When the skillet (or skillets) is hot, drizzle in enough oil to thoroughly coat the surface and increase the heat to medium-high. Place the chops in the skillet and press down firmly with a flexible spatula to make even contact with the pan. Cook, pressing down occasionally, until the underside is lightly browned, 3-ish minutes. Turn the chops over and press down again. Cook until the second side is browned like the first. Turn and repeat until the chops are gloriously browned and crisp on both sides, maybe two times in the hot seat for each side, 10 to 12 minutes total. (If you have a meat thermometer, aim for 135°F.) This frequent turning is an excellent way to build up browning on the surface of the chops while cooking them evenly internally. It's also convenient if you want to look busy and occupied while you gather your composure, or if you're trying to avoid a conversation with someone you live with, or if you're a shy hostess who likes having a job to do when people come over.

Once you're pleased with the browning, use tongs to perch the chops up on the outer edge and get some color on the fat. Transfer the chops to a plate and let them rest for 10 minutes.

Add the rice to the drippings in the pan and cook, pressing and tossing, until the rice is fluffy and starting to crisp, which shouldn't take too long. Season with salt and a few dashes of vinegar, then spoon into a serving bowl.

I like to cut the meat away from the rib bones, then slice it against the grain, ½ inch thick. Squeeze lemon wedges over, season with flaky salt, and serve, intact-family style, at the table along with the rice and chili crisp.

Market Meltdown

Some say that friend breakups are worse than romantic ones. Experiencing both at the same time is a third, even worse thing that I wouldn't wish on anyone—even my ex-friends.

A few months before separating, my husband and I bought a saltbox of a house, sixty-five miles from Brooklyn, in a town on the Long Island Bay where friends of ours also had summer/weekend places.

I can recgonize this decision for what it was: a last-ditch, valiant attempt to reverse the downward trajectory of our marriage. We tore out the wall-to-wall carpet in every room and demo'd the kitchen. By summer, the kitchen had been ripped down to studs, the bathrooms were untiled, and we were separated—house and marriage both in shambles. We paused construction and took turns staying at the house separately; it was livable, but barely.

Why go out there at all? For me, the beach was the draw, and it was a place I could stay at with a friend. But, in my squishy bits, there was also a possessive impulse to sleep there, as if I'd have no claim to the house later if I didn't log my time now. None of it was rational, but a mix of these motivations got me out of bed early on a hot Saturday in July. I knew that was when I had the best chance of running into folks I knew.

One of those people was a good friend, half of a married couple I'd spent lots of time with, who had stopped responding to my texts after I told her about the separation. As far as interpersonal signals go, silence is a strong one, but this was not my sanest era. *She's busy!* I thought. *Kids!* I thought. Each unanswered text spurred me to send another, and another, like repeatedly ringing the doorbell at a house with a light on upstairs, even though no one ever comes to the door.

An in-person chat would explain everything, I was sure of it. Iced coffee in hand, I hit the road, beelining it straight to the farmers' market. My timing was amazing. As I turned onto the narrow lane that led to the parking area, said friend was driving out, her husband at the wheel. I slowed to a near-stop. I saw them head-on, through my windshield and into theirs. Then, their car was inching alongside mine and I got a good look through the driver's window as they slowly rolled past me. *That's them,* I thought. Yet—no wave, no courtesy tap on the horn. *Oh,* I thought, reality descending on me. *Ohhhhhhhhhhh.*

I parked and killed the engine. I sat there for a few minutes, anxiously

Farmland near the farm stand during separation summer

sucking on melted coffee ice, back sweaty, driver door propped open for air. Finally: clarity. I understood. Getting divorced meant losing more than one relationship. I'd been dumped.

That said, I was at the farmers' market in high summer with—this just in—no other plans. I peeled myself off my car seat and went shopping. Sure, I had no friends, but I wasn't going to come all this way and miss out on melons! Melons make great friends! I can tell you everything I picked out while navigating the two short aisles packed with produce in rectangular crates: light green, pebbly-textured cucumbers; small shallots; locally made feta; a loaf of sourdough; plums and peaches; frilly little lettuces; garlic with bushy roots; and some diminutive, technicolor eggplant that I wanted to char and drag through labne.

With the beginnings of a meal assembling in my near-consciousness, I made the short trip to the regular supermarket nearby, where I was met by a huge display of precut watermelons wedges in Styrofoam packaging at the entrance. I called my sister from cookies and crackers, and stayed on the phone with her through hot sauces and vinegar. I recounted what happened that morning as a comedy routine for her, which everyone knows is the mature way to deal with hard feelings.

Back home, or whatever that place was, I unloaded my bags in the empty, hollow-sounding kitchen and bit into a wedge of watermelon, which was astonishingly tasty—sweet and crisp. Why wallow when you have all the ingredients for one of summer's greatest dishes? It was time for a watermelon and feta salad. I used a plastic knife to carve the watermelon into chunky pieces and moved them to a wide glass dish. The cucumber was more challenging to disassemble with disposable flatware. I ended up stabbing it halfway through and then cleaving off irregular pieces. I seasoned the watermelon and cucumbers with salt.

I lifted the feta from its container, which felt heavy with brine; it was sharp and salty and very fresh. I spent a while deciding exactly how to cut—or crumble!—the feta, using the time it took to make this dish as another emotion-avoidance strategy. Salad: fun. Feelings: bad. The cheese was wet and impossibly creamy. I broke it into clusters with my fingers, the

AUTHENTIC GREEK FETA

irregularity in line with the improvised shapes of the melon and cucumber. I poured some of the milky liquid from the feta over everything, grated a shallot on top, and added a zigzag of olive oil.

As I prepped, I wondered why I rushed to put watermelon—a fruit—into a salad, when I'd run screaming from any salad with a strawberry or blueberry in it. *Cucumbers and watermelon are both gourds,* I followed up, mentally bantering with myself. *That's why it's allowed.* Tomatoes are a fruit, too. I continued my alone conversation: *This would've been good with basil, or cilantro, or mint, or chives,* I thought. But I didn't have any herbs. *It would be good with some thinly sliced fresh chiles or pickled red onions,* but I didn't have either of those. *It would be good with a big pinch of Aleppo,* but there was no spice drawer to riffle through. I didn't have chairs or a table. I didn't have company, or my kids. I had two fewer friends than I had when I woke up, and a gut feeling that I wouldn't be the one cooking in this kitchen when the construction was done.

The salad I made that day

I picked up my lunch plate and walked out the back door to sit on a concrete step and eat. The backyard was filled with dappled light and I spotted a bunny nibbling grass at the edge of the lawn. I was right about one thing—it had turned out to be an epic day, weatherwise. I had a stoop to sit on, a plastic fork, crunchy cucumbers and juicy watermelon. When I finished the salad, there was a briny-sweet-oily dressing in the bottom of the bowl that was good enough to drink. So I drank it. I didn't have what I'd thought I had, but still—I had a lot.

Watermelon, Cucumbers, and Feta: Friends Forever
2 servings

½ mini seedless watermelon (about 2½ pounds, whole)

2 pretty little cucumbers

1 small shallot

Kosher salt

4 ounces feta in brine

Extra-virgin olive oil and red wine vinegar, for serving

Cut off the rind of the watermelon, then cut the flesh into randomly shaped pieces about 2 inches long. Transfer to a serving bowl. Cut the cucumbers into similarly sized pieces and add to the bowl with the watermelon. Thinly slice the shallot; let yourself cry. Add the shallot to the bowl and season generously with salt (the sweet watermelon and mild cucumber can take it). Pour in some feta brine and toss gently with your hands to combine.

Break the feta into large pieces and let them drop into the salad. Season with a few glugs of oil and several splashes of red wine vinegar; toss again to combine. Taste and adjust salt, brine, oil, and vinegar as desired.

Bittersweet Eggplant with Labne, Onions, and Honey
Serves 4 as a side dish

Kosher salt

2 pounds medium Italian, white, or graffiti (aka Fairy Tale) eggplants

Small-ish white onion

Pinch of sugar

3 lemons

2 teaspoons sherry vinegar

1 teaspoon Aleppo pepper, plus more

½ cup extra-virgin olive oil, divided, plus more

1 cup labne or Greek yogurt

1 garlic clove

Honey and mint leaves

Line a rimmed baking sheet with clean kitchen towels, parchment paper, or paper towels and lightly coat with a layer of kosher salt.

Peel the eggplant skin in alternating wide strips, creating a striped effect. Cut into ¾-inch-thick rounds, then set onto the salt in a single layer. Score the top side of each in a grid pattern. Sprinkle more salt over, then top with another towel. Set a cutting board or baking sheet onto the towel, then weight down with a couple of cans or jars of whatever. Let the eggplant sit for 15 minutes; this will season and tenderize it.

During this interlude, thinly slice the onion, then place in a medium bowl and season with salt and a pinch of sugar; toss to combine. Squeeze in the juice of 2 lemons (about ¼ cup), then add the vinegar. Season with 1 teaspoon Aleppo pepper and toss again. Let the pickle mixture do its thing while you cook the eggplant.

Heat a large skillet over medium-high. Working in 2 batches, pour ¼ cup oil into the skillet and arrange half the eggplant slices in the pan, without overlapping, scored-side down. Drizzle with a little more oil and cook, pressing down frequently, until the underside is very dark brown and charred in spots, 5 to 6 minutes. Turn over and cook until second side is similarly browned, another 5 minutes. Eggplant is greedy and thirsty. If the pan gets dry, it will scorch; add oil as needed.

Transfer eggplant to a plate and finely grate the zest of ½ lemon over while warm. Repeat with remaining ¼ cup olive oil, rest of the eggplant, and remaining zest.

Spoon the labne onto a platter and season with the juice of the zested lemon. Grate the garlic into the yogurt and stir to combine on the platter. Taste and season with salt and a big pinch of Aleppo.

Arrange the eggplant slices over the yogurt, then scatter the pickled onions on top. Drizzle honey over and top with a smattering of mint leaves.

Makeshift Kitchen Making Me Crazy

During separation summer, my teenage son got a job in the town where we'd purchased a beach house a few months prior, and my ex and I agreed to take turns staying out there with him for week-long stretches at a time.

The kitchen was in a stalled state of construction, with nothing but a fridge, a two-burner camp stove, a butcher block, and a plastic-legged slop sink. It was underequipped and unfinished, but the recipe developer in me thought it could be a fun challenge, a no-frills cooking experiment that was potentially good for content.

How hard could it be? Summer is the season of no-cook cooking, after all. I didn't have a dishwasher or an oven, but—as someone who had in fact once authored a magazine story about the cooking supplies to bring to your vacation rental—I knew what I'd need. I chose some knives and a couple of cutting boards from home, along with a starter pack of mixing bowls and wooden spoons, a pair of cast-iron skillets, and a tall pot. I was experienced, organized, and a little optimistic. I could pull off salads, pastas, quick-cooking proteins, and sautéed veggies. What I was not prepared for was the grief I'd experience for something that didn't yet exist.

The kitchen-in-progress would have been only the second of my entire married life. We moved to Brooklyn just months before our wedding in 1999, when I was still a line cook, and had lived there ever since. I wrote two cookbooks and made thousands of meals in it. When it came time to envision a new space, I had a lot of thoughts. I threw everything I had learned about kitchen design over the past twenty-plus years into the project: proper workflow; distinct zones for prepping, cooking, washing, and serving; which way the refrigerator door should swing; and how many steps I'd want to take before setting down groceries when I came in from the garage. (A garage! The city-schlepper's dream!) There was a true floor-to-ceiling pantry and a spot for *a stand-alone ice maker.* Ice! I was going to film cooking videos here, and thought about where we'd position cameras for the best angles. My ex and I talked about where it would feel most natural to have outlets for switching the lights on when you came in, and put more on the other side of the room for turning them off when you were heading up to bed.

CANADA DRY
SELTZER WATER

My therapist looked (uncharacteristically) aghast when I told him we'd bought a house, and the couples therapist we were seeing had a *lot* of follow-up questions about it, too. Each conversation with my ex about the budget left me in frustrated tears. Around that time, I relapsed on pot and kept it a secret from everyone, including my sister. The signs were compounding, data predictive of a colossal mistake unfolding at half speed. I chose not to deal. It was more entertaining to get stoned and focus on all the frozen margaritas I'd be making.

As it turned out, I wouldn't need all that ice. In April, a day after a fight that started in the cabinet showroom, we decided to separate. We broke the news to our children in May, the month we physically split. By July, I had made a handwritten list of my *real* friends, which I looked at often, seeking reassurance that I was not completely alone. In August, I was at the house with Cosmo, feeling insane for ever thinking I'd throw a party here for my birthday that month. Instead, I stood in the not-yet-a-kitchen and noted bleakly which pencil marks on the Sheetrock were for the refrigerator and which were for the overhead lights. I observed the way the afternoon light was going to fall on the dining table that didn't exist, and knew that if any family meals happened here, the table would be set for three, not four.

Instead of a toaster oven, I was cooking in an electric pizza oven that got up to 900°F (don't ask). My attempts at toast produced charcoal. I tried making a pork-and-potato frittata and ended up with hunks of rubbery meat and undercooked potatoes bound together by eggs that were both dry and somehow weeping. An attempt at Rice Krispies Treats—*a confection that children can make*—sent sticky strands of melted marshmallow into my hair and eyebrows. Bringing a pot of pasta water to a boil on the electric coil burner took over an hour, and trying to make the simplest sauce was a workout.

More than once, an exhausted Cosmo fell asleep waiting for dinner, couldn't be roused, and slept straight through the night. The only winning recipe that came out of that kitchen was a creamy green sauce made with random herbs in the fridge, which we dunked forkfuls of store-bought rotisserie chicken into.

If I'd actually been alone, I would have gotten the hell out of there. I hung in and feigned survival only because of my son. We sprayed ourselves down with bug spray and sat on the front steps to eat my mediocre meals. As I looked past the deep front lawn at the houses on the other side of the block, it started to sink in that those people would always be strangers to me, and that this house wasn't ever going to be my home. It was a place I was in, but not for long, the physical manifestation of a series of unfixable and unfortunate decisions.

Aside from my truly expert avoidance and procrastination skills, a cool thing about me is that my appetite is strong, daily dread notwithstanding. One day when Cosmo was at work, I got a craving for a tuna melt. As I mixed together the tuna salad, I mused about issues I had with the typical assembly—tuna on top of toast, cheese on top of tuna. My recipe developer brain got fired up. Melting the cheese warms up the tuna, which is not

Demolished

The first and last inverted tuna melt

ideal. I like a crunchy layer of romaine or iceberg between fish and cheese, but the broiler torches it—literally. *What if,* I said to the imaginary friend within me, *what if I melted the cheese on the bread, then put the lettuce on the cheese, then spooned the tuna onto the lettuce?* Hot gooey cheese on toast, intact lettuces, cold tuna. This! This is the kind of creative thinking a recluse with a pizza oven and a jar of tuna was capable of. I was onto something brilliant, for sure.

I toasted the toast at a sane temperature, then layered on a few slices of Muenster cheese and managed to melt them without scorching anything. I perched lettuce leaves on the cheese, cupped-side up, a crisp canoe. Then I spooned tuna salad onto the lettuces—temperature barrier intact—and took my inverted tuna melt to the al fresco seating area, aka the front step.

As they say on TV, what happens next will shock you. The shiny-smooth lettuce ribs slid across the cheese like a swimmer off an inflatable floatie. I tried to wrap my hands around the thing, and my fingers sank into the tuna salad in a decidedly unappetizing way. Taking a bite pushed one end of the lettuce down, the sandwich version of stepping on a rake and having the handle smack you in the nose with tuna. Fixing tuna melts was a cute premise, but there was no question that my solve was a fail. What's worse, my potential headlines were clunkers.

Tuna Melts: Fine the Normal Way

Deconstructed Tuna Melt: Actually Not Good

Don't Ruin-a Tuna

Dejected but hungry, I did what we'd done with every middling meal that week. I ate my mistake. The tuna and romaine became a lettuce wrap, which I ate like a ssam. That left me with a piece of cheesy toast. The bread was soggy and the cheese had congealed. Down the hatch.

My tuna melt was structurally unsound and conceptually flawed, but I refused to see defeat until a piece of damp, fishy lettuce smacked me in the face. You know what else I should have known better about? Buying this house when I knew I was unhappy. How a tuna sandwich got this message through to me, when therapists, siblings, and friends had failed, I don't know. But that ill-conceived sandwich was the fatal blow to my summer fantasy. I was ready to accept how bad of a situation I'd put myself in, punctuated by the rock-hard cement grinding into my butt.

I was missing my friends and family, and feeling cursed as a cook, but I had no regrets about trying. Now I recognize this as my style, this is how I learn, this is how I can be sure. The house represented something beautiful, a way to start fresh and figure out something new. But fantasies aren't real life—at least, not mine. I'd let myself fall for the idea of it, for what I wanted to be true. In the coming weeks, I would be able to admit to myself that I didn't even like it out there. Being okay with that was worth a lot more than bottomless ice. The truth was that I'd sold myself a shitty lunch. From that moment on, it got easier to let go. Continuing to hang on would have been as irrational as trying to love a bad sandwich. I could eat it that one time, but the next version would have to be better.

Green Sauce Saves the Day

Makes 3 cups

½ medium yellow onion, skin on

3 garlic cloves, smashed, skins on

Vegetable oil, for drizzling

Small handful of cilantro leaves and tender stems

Small handful of parsley leaves and tender stems

½ avocado

¼ cup fresh lime juice, from about 3 limes

½ spicy green chile, such as serrano, roughly chopped

2 tablespoons distilled white vinegar

Kosher salt

Ice cubes, as needed

3 tablespoons extra-virgin olive oil

Rub the onion and garlic with a little vegetable oil, then broil about 3 inches below the heating element until the garlic skins are charred and the onion is steamy and juicy, about 5 minutes for the garlic and 12 minutes for the onion (remove the garlic when it's done). Remove the garlic and onion skins. Roughly chop the onion.

Rinse and dry the cilantro and parsley, then very coarsely chop. Place the herbs in a blender with the avocado, lime juice, chile, vinegar, and 2 tablespoons water.

Add the cooled garlic and onion. Season with a large pinch of salt and blend on high speed until coarsely pureed (if the motor is having issues catching, add water a splash at a time until the blades spin).

Add a few ice cubes and continue blending until the sauce is smooth, creamy, and bright green. Taste and adjust seasoning with salt; the sauce can take quite a bit. Blend on medium while pouring in the olive oil; continue until green sauce is thick and emulsified. This sauce is best day of, but can be chilled airtight for 2 or 3 days; press a piece of plastic wrap against the surface to prevent oxidation.

Inverted Tuna Melt
Makes 2 open-faced sandwiches

2 celery stalks, cut into small dice

¼ red onion, cut into tiny dice

2 dill pickle spears, cut into small dice

2 tablespoons pickle brine

1 tablespoon distilled white vinegar

Kosher salt; freshly ground pepper

8 to 10 ounces canned/jarred tuna packed in oil, drained

1 tablespoon mayonnaise

1 tablespoon Dijon mustard

½ lemon

2 slices (¾-inch-thick) tight-crumbed bread

4 slices Muenster cheese

6 romaine lettuce leaves, rinsed and dried

Sriracha (optional)

In a medium bowl, combine the celery, onion, pickles, pickle brine, and vinegar, and season with salt and pepper. Stir and let sit for 5 to 10 minutes to lightly pickle the crunchy stuff.

Add the tuna and break it up with a fork until it is flaked to your satisfaction. Add the mayo, mustard, and juice of ½ a lemon. Season with salt and pepper. Stir until combined, then taste and adjust the mayo, mustard, and vinegar to your palate.

Toast the bread. Add cheese to each slice and broil until melted. Top with the lettuce leaves, rib-side down. Spoon the tuna salad onto the lettuce. Season with a few drops of Sriracha, if appealing, then attempt to eat the sandwich.

It will slide all over the place. It will be too juicy to be contained. Tuna salad may become airborne, so make sure you're eating over a plate. Your hands will get messy. The lettuce might free associate off on its own. A fork could be useful. You will wonder why the sandwich is assembled this way. It's a mistake. There are better ways.

The taste is good, though. Take what you've learned from the eating experience and apply it to the next tuna melt you make. Life is booby-trapped with things we need to figure out on our own; this sandwich is one of them.

The Pleasure of Not Feeling Guilty

I bet some total dipshit came up with the phrase "guilty pleasure."

The feelings that I associate with eating are, frankly, the best. Pleasure by the bushel. Joyful, kicked-back meals around empty platters, delicious-smelling food-stained napkins, a whole grilled fish in the center of the table picked to its bones, licking tears of laughter from your lips? I *definitely* want to eat that feeling. I remember finishing an ear of high-summer corn at a friend's house around the age of eleven, then watching wide-eyed as everyone else at the table sucked corn milk out of their denuded cobs. We didn't do that at my house. I felt a subversive thrill at the prospect, and then nirvana when I joined in. I'm grateful that girl didn't feel guilt about the noisy, utensil-free slurping going on around her, because the ecstasy of that moment is with me to this day.

Watching butter melt into toast

In the weeks and months following my separation, when I spent alternate weeks in the sublet apartment my ex and I shared, my emotions were hungry as hell. If what I was doing was eating my feelings, well, it seemed to me that the cliché could use an overhaul, too. With lots of solo time on my hands, I was flooded with memories of cooking for others and others cooking for me. The inch-thick piece of toast that my mom brought to my teenage bedside when I was sick, its surface spackled with butter that was slowly melting into the crumb. The can of Campbell's cream of mushroom soup I loved to make on Saturday afternoons in grade school, which my mom had taught me to dilute with whole milk rather than water, and that I seasoned with many pepper grindings. Or, eating leftover cobbler for breakfast on summer weekends, right out of the baking dish that had sat out on the kitchen counter overnight.

In the sublet, solaced by the patina on someone else's cast-iron pans and weathered cutting boards, I considered myself lucky for having an appetite. At the very least, it gave me something to do. I ate my way through loaves of crusty bread sliced thickly, griddled in olive oil, and topped with smashed avocados or jammy eggs, or shavings of Parm and chile

flakes, or all of the above. My tall turkey sandwiches pleased me, layered with crunchy lettuce, kimchi, cheddar, mustard, and mayo. Emotionally exhausted after hours-long lawyer calls, I defaulted to popcorn for dinner, happily and often. On winter weekends that felt both agonizingly short and impossibly endless, I would cook a personal pot of beans and greens for hours, then consume the entire batch in one nourishing sitting. I made cold Korean noodles with yet more kimchi, shaved celery, sticks of Asian pear, and hard-boiled eggs. I almost always had a 720ml bottle of silky-smooth sake in the fridge, which I couldn't find many reasons *not* to dip into, even after I'd been cautioned against drinking alone.

I found comfort in the act of making food, not just eating it. Cooking distracted me from the financial disclosure worksheets that had to be filled out, from missing my kids, from the fact that I needed to be intentional about social plans now that my family unit didn't make up my whole life. Eating was a daily necessity, and it was one of the few things I could do that I didn't feel guilty about (I saved my self-flagellation for when I slept until noon, then turned over to sleep some more).

Whenever I craved night cereal, I would have it, even if I was already showered, slathered, and in bed. Most people don't need a measuring cup and flaky salt for cereal, but I do. My composition consists of ice-cold rice milk and a crunchy cereal like Kashi GO or homemade granola (page 210), frozen blueberries straight from the bag, maple syrup, and a little salt. I've been honing this preparation for years; making it nice for myself is a key part of the appeal. The extreme coldness of the milk makes it hard to eat the cereal quickly, stretching the experience—layers of flavors and textures, the spoon, the bowl, the crunches, and the slurps.

Night cereal had the power to turn my mood around, even if temporarily. Inserting a wedge of regret into that craving/reward cycle would be the real crime. When I finished, I was content, taken care of. Decent upside for a woman who was picking the pieces of her life up off the floor—from a freaking bowl of cereal, no less. That truth earned it a spot along with so many other moments that were made better by what I ate, who I was with, and how I felt. There would always be a next time, and another food I could conjure up from my memories that would make my life feel full again.

Night Cereal
1 serving

Heaping cup of Kashi GO, Rice Chex, or Cherry-Cacao Granola (page 210)

Heaping ½ cup frozen wild blueberries or raspberries

About 1 cup rice milk or oat milk

Maple syrup and flaky salt, for seasoning

At night, combine the cereal and the frozen berries in a cereal bowl. Pour the rice milk into a measuring glass and add a few ice cubes. Stir until the milk is extremely cold. Pour the milk over the cereal, holding back the ice. Drizzle a few whispers of maple syrup over, then add a pinch of flaky salt. The best place to have this is in a quiet and peaceful night kitchen. Occasionally your ratio of cereal to milk might be off and it's nice to be able to adjust without making another trip. Sometimes you need a second bowl, and then you're right there. It's also very good to have if you're watching a show, and it's also nice to eat in bed if that feels right.

may all your
beans be
tender

Personal Pot of Beans and Greens

1 serving, potentially with leftovers

¼ cup dried beans, such as Calypso or cannellini

1½ teaspoons kosher salt, plus more for seasoning

Extra-virgin olive oil

3 garlic cloves, smashed

½ yellow onion, thinly sliced

Freshly ground black pepper

1 teaspoon coriander seeds

1 teaspoon fennel seeds

1 teaspoon Aleppo pepper

½ teaspoon ground turmeric

4 anchovy fillets

Parm rind (optional)

Big handful of torn escarole or kale

Bread, toasted or fried in olive oil, for serving

Sometimes you don't know in advance if you'll need personal beans, but if the thought occurs, soak the beans overnight in 6 cups of water that has been seasoned with 1½ teaspoons salt.

Heat a generous amount of olive oil in a medium pot over medium until shimmering. Add the garlic and onion and season with salt and pepper. Cook, stirring occasionally, until golden, about 5 minutes. Lightly crush the coriander and fennel seeds with a mortar and pestle, then add to the pot along with the Aleppo and turmeric. Cook, stirring, until the spices are fragrant and the vegetables begin to caramelize, 2 minutes or so. Add the anchovies and stir to break them up a bit.

Add the beans and their soaking liquid (if you didn't soak, add the beans with about 6 cups water and a big pinch of salt). If you have stock and prefer to use that, go for it. Drop in the Parm rind (if using). If needed, top off with enough water to cover the beans by about 1 inch.

Bring the mixture to a boil, then lower to a bare simmer. Taste the cooking liquid and add salt if needed. Delicious liquid is the key to delicious beans. Partially cover the pot and cook until the beans start to soften but are still a bit chalky in the center, 30 minutes or longer, depending on the bean and the soaking. Taste as you go and add more water as needed to keep the beans submerged.

Add the escarole and stir to submerge. Simmer gently until the beans are completely cooked through and the greens are soft and silky, 1 hour more. I like how the long-cooked greens transform the base of the soup. Add the escarole later, if you prefer a brighter flavor.

Fish out the Parm rind.

Serve the beans and greens drizzled with olive oil, with bread to the side for dips.

Things That Made Me Feel Free

Driving to the beach at whatever time. Nighttime walks with Marge. Being at the gym. Eating stand-up dinner. Laughing at dumb shit. Making new friends. Driving to Provincetown. Driving to Maryland. Driving over the Manhattan Bridge. Facebook Marketplace furniture adventures. Staying up super late. My nonmale friendships. Flying alone. Checking into hotels alone. Taking trains in Europe. Dancing in the living room by myself. Buying flowers. Keeping plants alive. Selling this book deal. Calling the plumber. Calling the HVAC guy. Using epoxy. Not responding to texts. Signing divorce papers in purple ink. Going to dance class. Boobs out at the beach. Kissing. Flirting. Sleeping in the middle of the bed. Not compromising.

2.
Ripe, Spicy, Sweet

mango
TWO DOLLARS
PAN CON TOMATE GUTS
tapioca
coconut
bitters orange
cointreau
Combine

your body is not a lemon
PRIDE. UNCONTAINED.
THINGS THAT
A BETTER IDEA:
a movie/show w/ Coz
for a walk w/ Marge
a menu
putting on a makeup look
making hot water
book
Diet Coke
NO SUGAR NO CALORIES
7.5 FL OZ (222 mL)
0 CALORIES PER CAN
178

Cruel, Cruel Avocado

There are plenty of nonscientific ways to predict what kind of day it's going to be—astrology, tarot, the chirp of birds. But nothing foretells my state of being like the inside of an avocado.

My heart has been broken a thousand times by at least that many avocados, but it's the few unblemished, pale-green, firm-yet-giving ones that keep the chase alive. Like a primo parking spot among the litter of tickets I've amassed. If only there were a reliable way to deliver a satisfying avocado experience. Sadly, there is not. Years of field research has proven that any avocado marketed as "ready now" is not ready. Not now, maybe not ever. Even among trained professionals, the success rate is shockingly low. I never met a food stylist who didn't arrive to set without four times the quantity of avocados needed for one shot. You're not going to find a ripe avocado for guacamole on Super Bowl Sunday, and definitely not on Cinco de Mayo. Are you insane? The hunting and gathering must commence several days in advance. How many days? No one knows.

I've bought organic and nonorganic. The very bumpy, reptile tail–textured ones and the smooth-skinned ones. The little ones, whose flesh is dwarfed by their pits. The very big ones, like bocce balls. Sometimes I've found bliss inside. When that happens: I drizzle the heavenly lobes with olive oil, pooling it into the place where the pit once was, season with salt and red chile flakes, and bury them under a blanket of nutritional yeast. Ideally eaten with a spoon right off the cutting board.

Perhaps you were counting on a glistening jade avocado to glamorize an ordinary pantry dinner of rice and beans (referred to as "mice and beans" in this family). Then this happens: brown stringy bits; caved-in hollow pockets; hard, watery flesh; bruises that remain, no matter how much is trimmed away. The disappointment feels routine. A two-dollar lottery ticket that didn't pay out. *Sorry, guys, I was going to serve this with avocado, but this one is no good.* It's a mistake we never learn from, a pothole of the produce world we feel in our gut.

I want so much to reveal how to tell when an avocado is ripe, but how could I, or anybody else, possibly know? Unlike a peach, tomato, or melon,

there is no sweet scent to indicate ripeness. Visually murky clues. A subtle, swampy array of colors, ranging from froggy green to bile-black. Wiggle the nub where the stem was attached? Obscene. Maybe they're more matte when unripe, and touched by a tiny sheen when ripe? Maybe!

We've been told that the flesh of a ripe avocado should give a bit when the skin is pressed. Terrible guidance. Untold amounts of personal avocado consumption have been squandered waiting for this moment to come, not to mention the bruises I left behind. The time to strike is when the avocado is still quite firm. You need to know this! Should you ignore the peak opportunity, what was once the avocado's apex could well be its grungy demise.

Like going on first dates time and again, buying an avocado requires blind optimism. From the rotating knife cut that splits the fruit from pole to pole, to the doorknob twist that separates one half from the other, the suspense is unmatched. The two sides come apart, tilted upward to meet your expectant gaze. If a spotted, chaotic camouflage awaits you—well, today's not your day. But if you behold an unbroken green-to-yellow ombre of buttery flesh, smelling of diluted lemon and distant grasses, with a pit eager to come out—this is the face card you hoped for on the flip. The memory of every ogre-ish avocado is wiped clean; your true love just pulled up. Whatever else comes at you today, baby, you're a winner.

What you want to see, times three

Quick Beans and Rice for When the Avocado Is Ripe

For 4

Vegetable oil

1 bunch scallions, cut into ¼-inch rounds

½ fresh chile, cut into small dice

Kosher salt; freshly ground pepper

1 teaspoon chile powder, such as chipotle

1 teaspoon coriander seeds, lightly crushed

2 (15-ounce) cans black beans, drained and rinsed

Chicken, mushroom, or vegetable bouillon paste or cubes (optional)

Handful of cilantro, with stems

Knob of butter

2 cups white rice, any type

Avocado, lime wedges, sour cream, and/or warm tortillas, for serving

To cook the beans, heat some vegetable oil in a medium saucepan over medium-high. Add the scallions and chile, season with salt and pepper, and cook until the vegetables are softened, a few minutes. Add the chile powder and coriander and cook, stirring, to bloom the spices. Add the beans, 2 cups water, and the bouillon paste/cubes, if desired (if not using, taste the liquid for salt).

Bring to a boil, then adjust the heat to maintain a gentle simmer. Partially cover and cook, stirring and tasting once in a while, until the liquid has reduced by about one-third and the beans are savory and delicious, 30-ish minutes.

In the meantime, get the rice going, Thinly slice the cilantro stems and leaves, separating them into two piles. Heat the butter in a 2-quart saucepot over medium until foaming, then add the cilantro stems and season with salt. Add the rice and stir to coat with fat; add more butter if needed to lubricate the rice. Pour in 2½ cups water and bring to a boil. Lower to the barest simmer, cover, and cook for 18 minutes. Add the sliced cilantro leaves and fluff the rice.

Serve the rice and beans with avocado, lime, sour cream, and/or tortillas.

Eating with Your Hands

European table manners were designed to keep chaos at bay. Dinner knives, when they came on the scene in the seventeenth century, had rounded ends, lest they were used as weapons at the king's table.

Cosmo and a bowl of something good

Makes a ton of sense. If you're going to sit down with a stranger from a faraway land who may or may not want to pillage your fiefdom, how they hold their utensil can tell you a lot about their intentions. Stab the grouse, not your dinner partner, know what I mean?!

Displaying "good" table manners is still a social signal of decorum, and eating "nicely" is something we (in North America, anyway) start training our babies to do as soon as they show dexterity with their little pincers. Bittersweet, isn't it? Why struggle to pick up macaroni with a fork when you had no trouble grabbing it with your fist? I, too, taught my children how to twirl their spaghetti and not to scrape their knives on their plates. But relying exclusively on handheld spikes and blades prevents us from having a more primal, sensory connection to our food. Whenever possible, I say ditch the utensils and go in with your hands, as people all over the world do as a rule.

It's a well-known fact that salads taste better when eaten by hand, and you can look very chic and demure if you use only your thumb and first two fingers to pluck lettuces. This projects a dainty energy, no matter the size of your digits. Anyone presented with chicken on the bone or brothy steamed mussels is obviously going in with their mitts. The highlight of my week is Saturday's car kimbap with my handy-dandy finger chopsticks, which I consume in the driver's seat before I give up my spot in front of H Mart. I don't hesitate to use my hands at restaurant tables and fancy dinners alike, which maybe isn't textbook manners, but as long as I keep vinaigrette off my clothes, I should be able to get away with it (n.b.: all of my shirts have vinaigrette stains).

What follows is a juicy salad comprising stone fruit and cured meat, with milky hand-torn mozzarella. It's ideal when the ingredients are around room temperature, and best if you are wearing next to nothing and sitting outdoors. A towel and a wet bathing suit would be good. You may

enjoy folding a strand of capocollo around a wedge of plum and dragging that through the vinaigrette before popping it into your mouth. You might enjoy dabbing both sides of the cheese into plum juices before it lifts off and heads to your face. I grant permission to scrub a pinch of flaky salt between your fingers, sending flurries onto a piece of plum and savor just that. Pressing torn bread into the liquids mingling on the plate? That should be done by hand.

Watch how relaxed and unabashed your friends become when they follow your lead. We're not crusading warriors, we're innocent children, uncorrupted by forks and unthreatened by our neighbors. While we pluck morsels out of our bowls, we keep our eyes trained on the faces around us, not on the knives in our hands.

Yes, I consider this a salad

Plums, Capocollo, and Mozzarella Hand Salad

Serves 2

8 ounces fresh mozzarella

2 ounces thinly sliced capocollo

2 tablespoons extra-virgin olive oil, plus more for serving

Balsamic vinegar, for drizzling

1 lemon, halved

Kosher salt; freshly ground pepper

3 medium plums

Flaky salt and Urfa biber, for seasoning

Baguette, for serving

Let the mozzarella and capocollo come to room temperature.

Pour 2 tablespoons oil into the bowl you're using to serve the salad. Drizzle in a bit of vinegar, then squeeze in the juice of ½ lemon. Season with kosher salt and pepper and taste. Adjust as needed with more vinegar and lemon; the dressing can veer on the acidic side to balance the richness of the cheese and the salume and the sweetness of the plums.

Cut the plums into ¾-inch wedges and add to the dressing, turning to coat. Tear the mozzarella into large pieces and arrange around the plums. Drizzle everything with more oil and season with a couple of pinches of flaky salt and Urfa biber. Drape and tuck the capocollo around. Serve with baguette.

Tomato (Gut) Feeling

My ex didn't like tomatoes, especially raw ones. *It's the gooey guts,* he said.

It became a running joke on my side of the family: a full-blooded Italian woman forced to decry the literal fruits of her Neapolitan ancestors' labor. From a Mediterranean diet perspective, the pillars of our union were doomed.

Tomatoes have never been gross to me, not in the slightest. But out of love and understanding and a desire to please him, I all but banished them from our table. Over time, I internalized the particularities of my lover's palate, drank the anti-tomato propaganda juice, and saw them as I imagined he did. The cherry tomatoes in my mom's rustic summer sauce cooked hot and fast till they burst and became saggy, gaggy fruit blimps. A platter of multicolored heirlooms morphed into obscenely gelatinous seed packets tethered to soft, boneless flesh. A crinkly broiled plum tomato served with roast chicken or grilled fish, intended to slip onto the fork with each bite—well, who would eat that? This was our forbidden fruit.

Tomato toast, gut-side up

If I found myself alone in my parents' kitchen with harvest from their tomato plants, I'd sprinkle coarse salt on a wedge and slurp the warm juices right from their fruity cenote. The seeds are slippery, and the amniotic situation they're suspended in is heavier than normal water; it's like aloe, like lake water, like whatever makes seaweed so slick. I get it—tomato innards are not for everyone, and having that treat in private minimizes the chances of grossing anyone out. But those textures, that anatomy, those fragrances, they are very much for me.

The summer after I separated, I did what I wanted, I ate what I liked, and I started to remember who I was. I let myself fall back in love with tomatoes, and by extension, accepted myself for the tomato slut that I am. I ate cherry tomatoes out of the pint container like berries. I left the B out of the BLT and squeezed thick-sliced beefsteaks to death between two slices of mayo-soaked bread. On a Facebook Marketplace adventure on Long Island, I went full paisan and sweet-talked the buyer's mom into giving me a jar of her homemade passata, dozens of which were neatly stacked in her garage but destined for my skillet.

It was tomato monomania. A tomato massacre. Guts were spilled. Shirts were stained. My tomato gluttony was a petty triumph in a summer otherwise full of loss. On market day, an array of skin-sniffed, hand-selected tomatoes lined my produce tray, full of potential, each one a cheap creative thrill, and all mine. To be clear—being alone *was* a thrill. An unapologetically messy, pulpy, seedy, sweet, juicy thrill.

Hot Garlic

Antis
SANTA
JULIA

Saucy Tomatoes and Chickpeas with a Sh*t-ton of Herbs
Serves 4

1 teaspoon coriander seeds

1 teaspoon fennel seeds

½ teaspoon cumin seeds

1 medium yellow onion

6 garlic cloves, divided

⅓ cup plus 2 tablespoons extra-virgin olive oil, divided

Kosher salt; freshly ground pepper

1 teaspoon sweet paprika

½ teaspoon crushed red pepper flakes

2 (15-ounce) cans chickpeas, drained and rinsed

¼ cup white wine vinegar

4 medium tomatoes, diced

1 cup packed chopped mixed tender herbs, such as cilantro and Thai basil

Zest of 1 lemon

Cooked jasmine rice, for serving

Lightly crush the coriander, fennel, and cumin with a mortar and pestle; set aside.

Mince the onion. Thinly slice 5 garlic cloves. Reserve remaining garlic for the sauce.

Heat a 2- to 3-quart saucepan over medium-high. Pour in ⅓ cup oil and add the onion and sliced garlic. Season with salt and black pepper and cook, stirring, until the onions are golden brown, 6 to 8 minutes (lower the heat if the garlic browns too quickly).

Reduce the heat to medium-low and stir in the crushed spices, then the paprika and red pepper flakes. Cook until fragrant, 1 minute. Add the chickpeas and cook, stirring to help release anything stuck to the pan (if necessary, add a splash of water). Season with salt and raise the heat to medium. Cook, tossing and stirring, until the fat is sizzling and popping in the bottom of the pot and the chickpeas are starting to look starchy, about 3 minutes.

Pour in the vinegar and reduce completely, 1 minute. Add the tomatoes and ½ cup water. Stir to combine, lower the heat to medium-low, cover, and cook until the mixture is slightly saucy and flavorful and the tomatoes have lost their shape, 15 to 20 minutes.

Meanwhile, put the herbs in a mortar; finely grate the lemon zest and remaining garlic over. Season with a large pinch of salt and pound until herbs and mixture look like wet grass, 2 to 3 minutes. Stir in the remaining 2 tablespoons olive oil and a splash of water. Taste the herb sauce and adjust seasoning. Serve the chickpeas over rice, with a spoonful of the herb sauce on top.

Pan con Tomato Guts
Serves 6 to 8

1 pound medium or large tomatoes

2 garlic cloves

2 teaspoons chili crisp

2 teaspoons extra-virgin olive oil, plus more for bread

1 teaspoon black vinegar

Kosher salt and MSG, for seasoning

2 baguettes (10 to 12 ounces each)

Flaky salt, for serving

Cut the tomatoes in half and grate the flesh into a medium bowl on the large holes of a box grater (you should have about 1½ cups). Finely grate the garlic into the tomato mixture, then add the chili crisp, 2 teaspoons oil, and the vinegar. Stir to combine, then taste and adjust seasonings with kosher salt and MSG.

Get ahead: The tomato mixture can be made up to 5 days ahead. Cover and chill.

Cut each baguette crosswise into 4-inch lengths, then split horizontally to create a top and bottom piece.

Heat a large cast-iron pan or griddle over medium until hot. Drizzle oil onto the cut sides of the bread, then place them in the pan, cut-side down, and lightly toast them, periodically pressing down on them to flatten, about 2 minutes. Turn onto the crust side just to warm, about 1 minute. Transfer the toasts to a cutting board.

Dividing evenly, spoon the tomato mixture onto the toasts and let it sit for a couple of minutes to absorb into the crumb. Cut each toast in half on the diagonal to create triangles. Season with flaky salt before serving.

Tomato and Cheddar Forever
Serves 4 to 6

2 pounds tomatoes, any types and sizes

Kosher salt; freshly ground pepper

Sherry vinegar, for seasoning

Extra-virgin olive oil, for drizzling

4 ounces sharp cheddar, grated on the large holes of a box grater

2 tablespoons unsalted butter

1 cup panko bread crumbs

1 teaspoon garlic powder

½ teaspoon sweet paprika

Slice the tomatoes ¼ inch thick if large and in half if small, and arrange on a platter. Season with salt and pepper, then douse with a few splashes of vinegar and drizzle generously with oil. Set the tomatoes aside to marinate at room temperature for up to 2 hours.

Line a large plate or baking sheet with paper towels. Heat a large cast-iron or nonstick skillet over medium heat. Add half of the cheddar in an even layer. Use a silicone spatula to tuck the edges in. Cook until the cheese melts and is golden brown, rotating the skillet as needed to cook evenly, 9 to 12 minutes. Season with pepper.

Use a thin spatula to lift up the cheddar frico, peeling it off the pan, and transfer it to the prepared plate. If it breaks into smaller pieces, it's no biggie—you're going to serve it in pieces anyway. Wipe out the pan and repeat with the remaining cheddar.

As it cools, the frico will become crisp. Break into large shards and transfer to a large bowl.

Wipe out the skillet and return to medium heat. Add the butter. When it's foaming, add the panko and season with salt. Stir to coat the panko with butter and cook, stirring almost constantly, until golden brown, about 6 minutes. Stir in the garlic powder and paprika.

Transfer bread crumbs to the bowl with the frico shards and toss to combine. Taste and adjust seasonings.

Gently turn the tomatoes over and spoon some of the accumulated juices over them. Top generously with cheddar crumbs. (You will have some left over; store airtight at room temperature for up to 2 weeks. Sprinkle them on green salads and simple pasta dishes, or use them to make this salad again.) Serve the salad with an extra drizzle of oil.

Cravings That Don't Go Away

Food cravings, like any other desire, should be honored. They're the body's way of transforming a physiological need into a conscious compulsion.

We are conditioned to think that to crave is to succumb to a physical weakness. That's wrong, nothing but a social construct. Eating is by definition carnal, and necessary. Listening to your body's wants is self-awareness on the most basic and beautifully babyish level.

What a special thing it is to want something and then have it. When else does that happen? I want a lot of things that I can't have: world peace, universal financial security, the ability to teleport. Those things are out of reach, which is why I answer my food cravings with a response as hard-wired as smacking my snooze button in the morning.

The summer of my separation, there were wildfires in Canada that blanketed New York in smoke and haze, and then a heat wave hit. The skies were orange, the temperature was oppressive, and the vibes were apocalyptic. All I could think about were chilled, wet, slippery foods—edible cold plunges. I did not stop myself. I braved sweltering subway rides into Manhattan's Koreatown seeking mul naengmyeon. I arrived sweat-drenched, wishing I'd brought a spare T-shirt. I sat and spooned up the frigid vinegary broth before the ice chips had a chance to melt, then slurped the chewy buckwheat noodles and nibbled on slices of Asian pear.

Other days, I drove to Xi'an Famous Foods in Williamsburg to dine solo on A1 Liang Pi, spicy chilled noodles tossed with bean sprouts and cilantro, and studded with squishy seitan. This seitan isn't anything like the rubbery blocks from my college days; it's floppy, built like a sponge, and absolutely saturated with chile oil dressing. I hadn't yet figured out a social life on my alone weeks. These little odysseys and the transactional contact that came with them made me feel less isolated. I returned to the apartment happily full and feeling slightly more human.

The need to pass the time was constant, and a newfound obsession for cold tapioca in coconut milk entertained me at the sublet. I didn't think about why I needed this or where the urge came from; I simply submitted.

The noodle dish I think about the most

Before it was a recipe: something I felt compelled to eat

Every curvy hallway of my brain led me back to tapioca and coconut desserts. I consumed a stream of how-to videos on YouTube, salivating over Thai sago soups, Chinese taro and tapioca puddings, and Filipino "mango bango" before attempting an approximation at home. I became fixated on dialing in the aromatic coconut base, seasoning it with salt and sugar, and tasting it while the lemongrass, mint, and ginger infused to figure out how long the herbs took to bloom. Simmering the tapioca beads was easy, and the tiny clear orbs felt bouncy between my fingers in the colander as I rinsed and cooled them. I tried berries and cherries on top, but I preferred musky diced mangos and the innards scooped from magenta passion fruits. Fridge-cold wasn't cold enough that summer. Every night I made sure that the old-timey metal ice cube trays were filled with water and back in the freezer, poised for duty.

I kept the pearls and the coconut base separate in the fridge and brought them together whenever the mood struck, which was every day for about ten days. Before I served the sweet soup to myself, I'd wrap a couple of ice cubes in a kitchen towel and smack them with a metal spoon until they broke into big shards. Assembly happened in a white enameled bowl: a mound of tapioca swimming in coconut broth, topped with juicy spoonfuls of fruit, ice tucked to the side. I ate it with a tiny spoon to make it last longer, and if the heart wanted more, I composed a second bowl.

Everything about this dish is high femme—the shimmering tapioca pearls, the sunrise palette of oranges and pinks, the sweet opalescent soup, my filigreed spoon, the sparkling ice crystals. Eating it was an antidote to the atmosphere of monstrous smoke and dank sweat outside my window. The springy little beads, almost devoid of flavor, rolled around like fairy caviar on my tongue. The frosty, just-sweet-enough coconut soup was precisely what every tropical suntan lotion wishes it smelled like. It seems so obvious now why I craved it. It was a tiny treat, dessert fit for a wee maiden, a princess, and I was an angel for giving it to myself right when my heart was engulfed in flames. Within a few days, the smoke had dissipated and I wasn't circling around ice-cold tapioca anymore—the need satisfied or extinguished. Which one, I don't know. But in the moment, she was my everything.

You're so perfect, I told my tapioca.

That was so sweet of you, I told myself.

Must-Have Coconut Tapioca with Tropical Fruits
6 to 8 servings

1 lemongrass stalk, trimmed, tough outer husk removed

Thumb-size piece fresh ginger

1 (13.5-ounce) can unsweetened coconut milk

1 cup rice, almond, or oat milk

½ cup sugar

Handful of mint sprigs

Kosher salt

1½ cups small tapioca pearls

Ice, for serving

Diced mango and/or passion fruit, for serving

Trim the lemongrass, then use the blunt edge of your knife to give it several good whacks down the length to release the essential oils. Cut the lemongrass into ¼-inch pieces. Slice the ginger about ¼ inch thick and then use the broad side of the knife to smash and flatten it so that the fibers tear apart.

Place the lemongrass and ginger in a small pot with the coconut milk, rice milk, sugar, and mint, squeezing the mint in your palm as you go. Add ¼ cup water and a pinch of salt and bring to a simmer, stirring to help dissolve the sugar. Turn off the heat, cover the pot, and let it steep at least 30 minutes and up to 2 hours.

Strain the coconut base, pressing on the solids to eke out every drop, then cover and chill (you can do this several days in advance, if you wish; refrigerate until ready to use).

Cook the tapioca in rapidly boiling water with a pinch of salt, stirring often, until still chewy but not chalky in the center—check package for time estimates (the brand I use takes 15 minutes). Pour through a fine-mesh strainer, then run under cold water, raking with your fingers, until the pearls are cool. Shake off excess liquid and use immediately, or cover and chill for up to 4 days.

For each serving, spoon ½ cup tapioca pearls into a small bowl and add about ¼ cup coconut base. Wrap the ice in a clean kitchen towel and whack with a metal spoon or rolling pin to break into large shards. Add a few pieces of ice to the tapioca, and top with a large spoonful of fruit.

Reasons to Have Chips in the House

One thing about going through a separation in the summer—you get so thirsty!

And not for water. Or nudes (that came later). My taster was up for items with a high ABV: sake, gin, tequila, mezcal. It wasn't my healthiest habit, but it happened.

When I worked in restaurants, I learned that loud dining rooms fuel the desire for salty, fatty things. With one sense overwhelmed, another will raise its voice, seeking feedback, searching for proof of life. Hearing blown out, the palate finds stimulation in fried mozz, hot sauce–soaked wings, caviar bumps. The salt, in turn, reignites thirst—*Yes, waiter, another round.* Inebriated people overorder. Snack, drink, snack, drink—next thing you know, check averages are *way* up. The noisier the better—at least when the bottom line is concerned.

Being on an airplane has a similar effect. Eventually we dull to the engine's roar, visuals dimmed when the window shades are pulled closed. Foods with a sane amount of salt can't cut through the noise. Normal flavors taste bland. When else would you suck down a can of Bloody Mary mix, trying to feel something, anything? Chex Mix hits like a bag of sticks up there, fueling a hunt for stimulus. We suck roasted peanut dust off of our fingers, and our brains can barely detect a dot of honey.

By myself every other week, the house may have been quiet, but emotions were at full volume. For me to feel relief, the antidotes needed to be equally loud and electric. This was no time for fluffy piña coladas or syrupy Aperol spritzes. Stark contrast would cut through the slog. I chose the cocktail equivalents of splashing cold water on my face. The grown-up bitterness of a G&T was an anchoring slap on the back. I licked salt off the rim of my mezcal margarita and held it on my tongue, sipping smoke. I learned to love 50/50 martinis, specifically the Eventide—one part gin, one part Cocchi Americano. I stirred the liquids with ice and bitters until they became sluggish with freeze. If I served the drink in a coupe, it slipped right down my gullet. Putting it on the rocks mitigated my consumption (a bit).

It didn't have to be alcohol for me to become fixated. I got out the electric juicer to replicate my mom's famously sour lemonade, savoring the pucker from my cheeks to my eyebrows. On New York City's most disgustingly hot and humid days, I chugged Fresca spritzers from quart containers rattling with ice: brain freeze hurt so good.

My at-home appetizer menu tragically did not include jalapeño poppers, but I had other salted suitors on my roster. As crunchy as possible, please, to mute the static of financial worry and echoes of nasty phone calls that played on a loop in my head. Would aggressive snacking combat the maternal guilt I felt for choosing a life that reduced time with my children by half? No, but at least it was distracting. I worked my jaw through thick contorted kettle chips, seed-studded pretzel chips, mini Triscuits, cheddar Ruffles, Stacy's Pita Chips, and Cool Ranch you-know-whos. Fritos: lowbrow brilliant. Classic Lay's: a sodium showdown. The range of possibilities in a good bag of totopos was always enticing. Pretzel rods? Magic wands.

To paraphrase Elaine Benes, the pretzels were making me thirsty. Good thing there was a frosty glass in my hand. Each sip of drink brought relief to a tongue parched and tingling from salt; cold and crunchy paired up like Frog and Toad as I nibbled and gnashed my way through the rewrite of my life.

Chips and a cocktail can do all that? It's just a bevvie and a snack. But it was enough to get me out of my head and back into my body—well-seasoned and properly quenched.

G&T, Baby
Makes 1 cocktail

2 ounces London dry gin

Kosher salt

Angostura bitters

1 lemon

Ice

6 to 8 ounces chilled tonic water

Pour the gin into a highball glass and add a wee pinch of salt and a few dashes of bitters. Beginning at the stem end of the lemon and working around the fruit, use a vegetable peeler to remove the peel (without pith) of all but one-quarter of the lemon, ideally in one long strip.

Lightly twist and bend the peel over the drink to expel citrus oils, then rub the peel around the rim of the glass. Drop the peel into the glass, then fill with ice. Top off with the tonic water. Slice off a portion of the lemon that still has its peel. Squeeze in the juice, then drop the lemon wedge into the beverage. Serve with a cocktail stirrer or a straw.

My Completely Perfect Mezcal Margarita
Makes 1 cocktail

Kosher salt

1 fat lime wedge

Ice

2 ounces mezcal

¾ ounce fresh lime juice

½ ounce agave

½ ounce Cointreau

3 dashes orange bitters

Pour a thin layer of kosher salt onto a small plate or saucer. Lightly rub the lime wedge onto half of the rim of a rocks glass, just to moisten. Invert the glass onto the salt to coat. Fill the glass with ice.

Combine the mezcal, lime juice, agave, Cointreau, and bitters in a cocktail shaker. Fill the shaker with ice. Cover and shake enthusiastically and noisily until the hand touching the cocktail shaker seems like it is going to freeze and fall off. Do not stop until the risk of physical injury seems real. Two or three shakes is insulting to the spirit of margaritas everywhere and worse than that, the drink just won't be as good.

Strain the margarita into the salt-rimmed glass and serve with the lime wedge.

A Less-Lethal Martini
Makes 1 cocktail

1½ ounces Cocchi Americano

1½ ounces London dry gin

Orange bitters

Ice

Orange or lemon twist

Pour the Cocchi and gin into a cocktail shaker, pint glass, or glass jar. Sprinkle in a few dashes of orange bitters. Add a handful of ice and stir until the drink is extremely chilled and nicely diluted—taste it along the way. Strain the cocktail into a coupe glass and serve it up or pour into a rocks glass filled with ice. Garnish with a twist in either case.

Sour Patch Lemonade
Makes 1 quart

4 lemons, plus wedges for serving

⅓ to ½ cup sugar

1 cup very hot water

Kosher salt

Citric acid (optional)

Ice

Use a vegetable peeler to remove the zest (without pith) in wide strips from 2 lemons. Drop the zest into a blender along with the sugar (start with ⅓ cup if you like a barely sweet lemonade; you can always add more). Pour the hot water into the blender to melt the sugar. Let that sit while you prep the lemons.

Cut the peel and pith away from all 4 lemons, then cut or tear the fruit into quarters or sixths, popping out the seeds as you go. Discard peels. Add lemon flesh to the blender along with 3 cups cold water and a pinch of salt. Blend on high speed until liquefied, then pour through a fine-mesh sieve into a pitcher or large jar, pressing firmly on solids. Taste the lemonade and stir in more sugar if your palate wants it. Season to taste with citric acid, if using.

Serve over ice with a lemon wedge.

Seltzer, Fresca, Seltzer
Makes 1 large beverage

Ice

About 20 ounces cold seltzer or club soda

1 (7.5- or 12-ounce) can Fresca, chilled

Grapefruit, orange, lemon, and/or lime wheels (optional)

Fill a 1-quart container or other drinking vessel three-quarters of the way with ice. Add enough seltzer to come about one-third of the way up the side of the container. Pour in the Fresca (hold a few ounces back if you have the bigger can). Top off with more seltzer. Garnish with citrus wheels, if desired.

mr. mango
STRINGBEAN
59¢
BRUSSELS SPROUT
199
SCALLION
1.00
OCEAN MIST
GREEN ONIONS
OCEAN MIST
GREEN ONIONS
OCEAN MIST
GREEN ONIONS
SF70

929-

3.
Learning Curve

Pancakes
Rd #1
3 min first si
add some sugar
#2 increased powder by ½
over
2/2
GOOD STOCK 2/6
Lobster Spicy Mayo
mayo
sambal

2½ lbs chicken
salt
veg oil
2 med onion
6/8 garlic
spices?
coriander
mushroom
pinch
1/4 cup cider vin
2 cans
chipotle in a
coconut milk
sour cream?
avo
tortillas?
raw onion
season chix
preheat
oil / add
remove chix / 14-16
add onions
stir + s
cover /
10 mins add
garlic
5 cloves
smoked
NOODLES

Carole's Soup, My Soup, Leo's Soup

I grew up eating my mom's pasta e fagioli, a Sunday staple. When I moved into an off-campus apartment during college, I craved it like crazy and called her—Carole—up to find out how to make it.

At first, I was very loyal to her tomatoey recipe, motivated to match the taste memory if I could. Only later I found the confidence to tweak and change it a little bit here, a little bit there. My interpretation of her recipe, which we call "fazool," despite the fact that my mom has never liked that moniker, is the one my kids have grown up on. Less tomato, lots of anchovy. The core of the dish—pasta and beans—is the point, and I honor that.

We're now in the third generation of the recipe, figuratively and literally: My older son, Leo, texted me for the instructions last year, when he started cooking for himself at college. I about fell to the ground and wept with joy when I saw his message. Leo's fazool is similar to my version, but he has incorporated his own special touches. His house, his fazool.

While writing this book, Leo shared his technique with my mom, and she had thoughts on the changes *he'd* made—namely, that she was looking forward to the day he comes over and cooks it for her. Before the three of us, my Italian ancestors, most of whom are nameless to me, were also making pasta e fagioli. I like to think their children replicated their methods and used the same ingredients, chasing consistency just like we do. People won't remember what you did or what you said, but they'll remember how your soup made them feel—is that how that quote goes?

Even though I changed Carole's and Leo changed mine, each version is correct and right and perfect. And that's the thing: A pot of pasta and beans is unique to the cook who makes it, and the people who get to eat it will love that bowl the most. It's never the same, but it's always good.

Leo: I never met a fazool I didn't like, but my preference is for maximalism. I like as many things in fazool as possible. I have little to no interest in an Italian wedding soup or a minestrone. I don't want boiled things. I want thickness. I want suspension.

You make it on Sunday because you don't go anywhere else after you eat it. I start with cannellini beans. And definitely ham hock. If it was up to me, I would put three ham hocks in it. (I recently did two hocks for soup for six people.) And I add so much pasta. So much pasta that it's almost like a bowl of pasta, not soup. A pound of pasta—rigatoni—for two people. When I make it at school, it tastes like yours, but the biggest difference between our recipes is the ratios. I add more beans, soffritto, and pasta.

The thing is, you can make two fazool at the exact same time, with the exact same ingredients, and have them taste totally different.

Carole: Well, I wouldn't dismiss minestrone, which is a very large category, in and of itself. That aside: One thing Leo uses in his that I never used in mine is fennel, and the next time I make a batch, I'd like to try that. I also think it's interesting that he blends a portion of the soup with an immersion blender and gets more of a puree before putting it back in. I always use my Cuisinart, which isn't the same.

I don't make mine the same way every time—none of us do—but I would closely follow his. I would like to at least experience it the way he intends. Or, even better, maybe on Thanksgiving weekend, also known as turkey sandwich weekend, he could make it for us. That would be a perfect thing for lunch on Sunday.

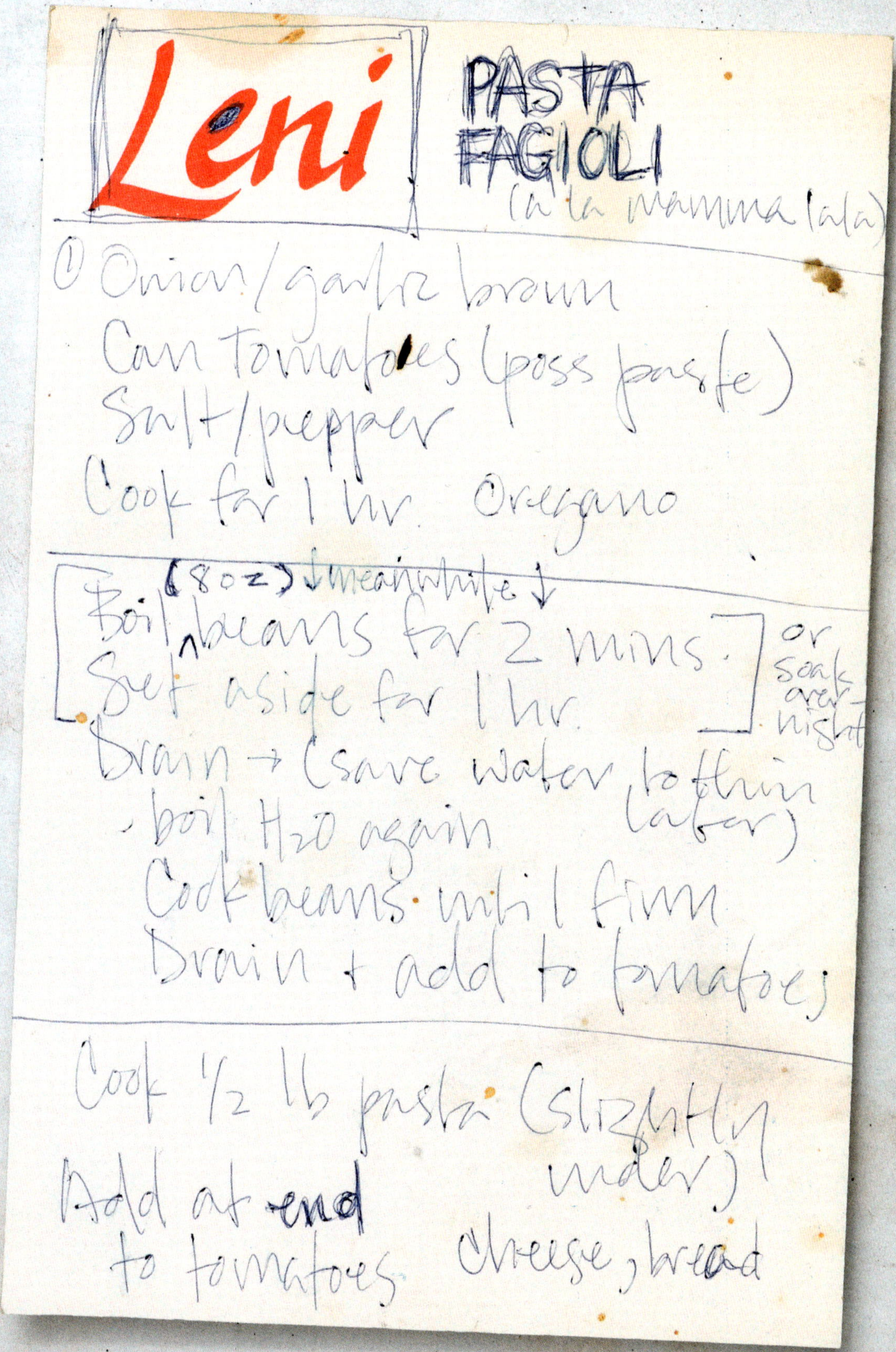

Leni

PASTA FAGIOLI
(a la mamma lala)

① Onion/garlic brown
Can tomatoes (poss paste)
Salt/pepper
Cook for 1 hr. Oregano

[Boil (8 oz) beans for 2 mins. ↓meanwhile↓
Set aside for 1 hr.] or soak over-night
Drain → (save water to thin later)
boil H2O again
Cook beans until firm
Drain + add to tomatoes

Cook ½ lb pasta (slightly under)
Add at end to tomatoes
cheese, bread

Carla's Chovy-Forward Fazool
8 servings

8 ounces dried beans, such as baby lima, gigante, Corona, or cranberry beans

Kosher salt

For the Soffritto

6 garlic cloves, peeled

1 large yellow onion, halved

1 fennel bulb, stems trimmed, roughly chopped

4 carrots, peeled and roughly chopped

½ cup extra-virgin olive oil, plus more for serving

Kosher salt; freshly ground pepper

6 anchovy fillets

2 teaspoons dried oregano

2 teaspoons fennel seeds

½ teaspoon cumin seeds

½ teaspoon ground turmeric

2 teaspoons mild chile flakes, such as Aleppo, plus more for serving

¼ cup tomato paste (double concentrate)

For the Soup

Kosher salt; freshly ground pepper

3 bay leaves, fresh or dried

2 dried shiitakes or porcini

1 bunch of kale, leaves torn into 3-inch pieces

1 or 2 Parmigiano rinds (optional)

8 ounces small ridged pasta, such as orecchiette or cavatelli

Parmigiano and toasted or fried crusty bread, for serving

To soak your beans before cooking, put them in a bowl with 1 tablespoon salt and 6 cups water and leave them at room temperature for up to 24 hours. This step is not required, but it shortens the cooking time for the beans and preseasons them.

Make the soffritto:
In a food processor, pulse the garlic, onion, and fennel until finely chopped. Transfer to a large bowl. Pulse the carrots in the processor until finely chopped and add to bowl with onion mixture. If you don't have a food processor, chop the vegetables by hand, as finely as patience will allow.

Heat a 6-quart Dutch oven or other large heavy pot with a lid over medium. Add the olive oil. When the oil is hot, add the chopped vegetables. Season generously with salt and pepper, stir to combine, and cook until the vegetables are bright and start to release their liquid, about 3 minutes.

Cover the pot and reduce the heat to medium-low. Cook the soffritto, checking and stirring every 5 to 10 minutes, until the vegetables have released a lot of liquid and become very soft, without taking on any color, 20 to 25 minutes.

Continue to cook, covered, stirring more frequently, until the soffritto has lost at least half its original volume and is just starting to brown, about 15 minutes more.

Uncover and cook until the soffritto is orangey-brown in color and starting to fry in the oil, which indicates the vegetables have given up all of their liquid. (The math is right: Cooking the soffritto takes about 40 minutes, which is why this soup tastes so good.)

Scoop out half of the soffritto and transfer it to a storage container. Let cool, then freeze for the next batch of soup or beans; setting it aside before you add the anchovies and other seasonings means you can adjust it to complement whatever dish you're making in the future.

Add the anchovies, oregano, fennel seeds, cumin seeds, turmeric, and chile flakes to the remaining soffritto in the pot. Cook, stirring, until the anchovies have disintegrated, about 2 minutes. Add the tomato paste, stir to coat, and cook until the paste has darkened by a couple of shades, about 3 minutes more.

continued

Finish the soup:
Add the beans, along with their soaking liquid. (If using unsoaked beans, add 2 quarts water and 1 tablespoon salt.) Drop in the bay leaves and shiitakes, then add water to cover the beans by 2 to 3 inches. (If you have homemade chicken or vegetable stock on hand, you can use it instead of water, but it's not necessary, flavor wise.)

Bring the mixture to a boil over medium-high and season with salt and pepper. Reduce the heat to a gentle simmer, partially cover the pot, and cook, stirring every 20 to 30 minutes or so, until the beans are tender but not completely cooked through, 1 to 2 hours, depending on your beans (add water as needed to keep the beans submerged by 2 inches).

Stir in the kale and Parm rinds (if using), partially cover, and cook soup with lid askew, stirring occasionally, until the beans are completely soft and kale is silky, 30 to 45 minutes more. Taste periodically and season as needed. If the beans are being stubborn and the kale ends up cooking longer, it's all good.

Transfer about 3 cups soup mixture (without rinds) to a tall container and blend with an immersion blender until smooth (or do this in a stand blender). Stir the puree into the soup.

Cook the pasta in a pot of well-salted boiling water for 2 to 3 minutes less than the time indicated on the package. Drain the pasta, add it to the soup, and cook until the pasta is al dente, about 2 minutes. Taste and adjust seasoning.

Serve the soup drizzled with olive oil, with Parmigiano for grating over, bread for dunking, and more Aleppo.

Renato's Copper Pans

My mom, Carole, was born in New Jersey in 1942 and was the big sister to her brothers, Renato and Carlo.

Their father died of lymphoma in 1946, and my grandmother, Nana Lea, raised them as a single mom on a secretary's salary. The siblings navigated their less-than-privileged upbringing, working their way through college and into lifestyles that seemed like a long shot when they were young. Renato became an art dealer, eventually opening his own gallery, Danese, which is where he worked until his death from cancer in the spring of 2020.

My childhood image of Renato is as a mustachioed, bespectacled, and charming bachelor who always smelled good. My sister called him Nocky when she was little and the nickname stuck; soon the whole family referred to him as Nocky or Uncle Nock. Renato was charming and affectionate and loved to laugh. Without daughters of his own, he was loyal and protective of me and Nina, in a "no one could ever be good enough for you" Italian uncle kind of way. The first time he met my not-yet-husband, he immediately put him on the spot, asking, *What are your intentions with my niece?* It was too cute to be embarrassing, and I let my ex navigate that one on his own.

Renato's adult life was filled with nice things—antique furniture, modern art, songbirds in ornate cages hanging in the kitchen alongside his gleaming copper pans. He was very particular about his belongings. Very. Even as a teen, I was forbidden from touching his stereo, especially the volume dial. No one who came over for holiday meals was asked to clear the table, but not because he didn't want us to get up: he wouldn't risk one of us chipping the china. Instead, he washed every plate by hand after we left.

Years later, Uncle Nock and Aunt Christina (his second wife) moved from Manhattan to southern Rhode Island. Amid purging and packing, Christina called and asked if I'd like his collection of vintage copper pans, which bore the stamp of the famed Parisian cookware shop, E. Dehillerin. To my shocked *Are you sure??????* she said: *They're big and heavy and collecting dust here. I'm not moving them to Rhode Island, where there's no chance we'll suddenly start cooking with them. If you'll use them,* she said, *they're yours.*

She didn't have to ask me twice.

I took the whole inventory: two lidded 4-quart saucepans, one with straight sides, the other flared; a daintily proportioned 2-quart pan with shallow, straight sides; and a stunning wide rondeau with a lid like a cymbal. The long iron handles arch upward dramatically; they're 3 inches thick at the base and are looped at the end, meant to be hung above a hearth or range. The handles are secured to the pans with beefy, raised rivets. The material is a little more than 3mm thick—as good as it gets—and the surfaces boast the glossiest, most buttery stainless steel I've ever seen. Each was far nicer than any equipment I owned, and I had some nice shit. They don't make them like they used to, literally—including at E. Dehillerin.

The first thing I cooked in the big rondeau was a mess of feathered maitake mushrooms from the farmers' market. I didn't do anything out of the ordinary—just my usual olive oil, salt, and pepper, threw in a few thyme sprigs and smashed garlic cloves toward the end. But the way the moisture from the mushrooms created friction as it evaporated, sputtering and bouncing as it hit the glass-like surface, was thrilling. When the mushrooms were crisp, they slid around the pan like a granny on black ice. The lump of cold butter I tossed in to finish them off skidded from one side to the other, liquefying and foaming as it went. *You,* I said to the pan, *are not like the other girls.* I snapped a pic and texted it to Renato so he'd know his copper was happy with its new family.

Duck leg island, duck fat sea

I sat down at some point and wrote him a "proper thank-you note," as my mom would say, because he was old-school and would appreciate it (my text didn't count). I don't remember anything I said, to be honest. But I have no trouble remembering all the ordinary ways I've cooked in those pans, from reheating soup to frying leftover rice. I make duck confit in the small one: four duck quarters fit perfectly, thighs pressed against the outer edge, ankle bones crossed daintily in the center. The duck gets lightly coated with spices, ruddy flesh studded with cold nuggets of fat. It cooks in a low oven overnight; the renderings become the cooking medium, thinning the skin to a crisp and morphing the thigh muscles into delectable shreds. Some French lady would have used copper pans like these to make duck confit in a waning hearth; I use the cozy and efficient confines of my toaster oven, and it comes out amazing.

The rondeau is wider than my biggest Dutch oven, and the high, straight sides protect my range and countertop from grease splatter. This makes it an obvious choice for browning a batch of eight bone-in chicken thighs and for building the chipotle-spiced coconut milk sauce they braise in. It's my first pick for pasta sauces because when the sauce is done, the pan easily contains the noodles along with the vigorous tossing that sends pasta water flying up the sides of the pan. When spring market trips lead to having five types of spring alliums in the house, I will happily watch a mountain of them cook down and caramelize, flavored with lemon and butter. That, as a pasta sauce? Get outta here.

The one thing I've never done with these pans is polish them. They hang from a massive marble pegboard wall that I built into my kitchen when I renovated, just a few months after Renato was gone. I love looking at their weathered undersides, seeing their vintage-penny color alongside the matte black of my cast-iron skillets. I love feeling their weight in my arms when I lift them off their hooks. I love that my children aren't afraid to choose them to boil water for ramen or reheat leftovers; they know these pans belonged to their great-uncle, and they know that their preciousness is a reason to reach for them as often as possible.

Renato was proud of me when I published my first cookbook, but he wasn't around when the second one came out. I promised to use these pans when I took them home, not knowing at the time they were an early inheritance. He didn't get to see his copper hanging on my kitchen wall, but he would have appreciated the design choice. He didn't get to watch the videos I made cooking pasta dishes with them, which is a real fucking kick in the nuts. I think about him every time I set his pans on the stove, touching the same handle he touched. The pans are made to last a lifetime, and I'm determined to get full use out of them on the daily, since none of us knows how long our lifetime will last.

Renato would be happy knowing his copper will never collect dust in my house. (Christina sure is!) He would not, however, approve of my failure to polish them—in fact, I wouldn't hear the end of it. But, this is how we are different. If using them meant polishing them, I'd never use them. As far as I'm concerned, these objects transcend space, time, earth, and the heavens.

Renato loved art, he appreciated beauty, he cared about how things were made, and he felt a responsibility to care for his belongings. If he were still here, I'd host him for a dinner, cooked in his copper. I know he'd get a thrill out of that. And after the meal was done, he'd find a way to sneak off to the kitchen and polish the pans himself, because they would look so much prettier on the wall like that.

Dreaming of Duck Confit
For 4; easily scaled up

4 Pekin (Long Island) duck legs, thawed if frozen

Kosher salt

A few whole dried chiles, such as er jing tiao, pasilla, or cascabel

Palmful of aniseed or fennel seeds

1 or 2 whole star anise or a cinnamon stick

A few dried juniper berries or palmful of coriander seeds

¼ cup warm duck fat, schmaltz, rendered pork fat, and/or room-temperature extra-virgin olive oil, plus more as needed

A day or two before making the confit, score the skin of the duck legs, being careful not to go all the way down to the flesh. Cut a few slashes into the fatty pocket on the flesh side of the thigh as well, to help the fat render. Season the duck on both sides with kosher salt, rubbing it into the skin. Transfer to a bowl or baking dish where the legs will fit snugly and add the chiles, aniseed, star anise, and juniper and toss to distribute the seasonings. Cover and chill for up to 2 days.

Preheat the oven or toaster oven to 275°F.

Choose a heavy-lidded pot that's just big enough to accommodate the duck in a single layer—copper, if you're lucky. Pour in ¼ cup water and ¼ cup fat. Arrange the legs in the pot, skin-side down. A little overlap is okay; they'll shrink as they cook. Cover the pot and bake for 1 hour. The legs should be about halfway submerged with fat.

Turn them skin-side up and add more fat as needed to come up halfway. Cover the pot and do something else for 6 or 8 hours, such as going to sleep for the night.

When done, the drumstick bones will wiggle freely in the joint, perhaps dislocating completely if twisted and tugged. The skin should be browned, with most of the fat rendered, and the flesh will flake and shred apart easily. Eat while warm, or transfer to a clean container and strain the rendered fat over. Let cool, then cover and refrigerate for up to 10 days.

To reheat the duck, warm it gently in its fat over low heat. Or, to serve it with crispy skin, cook it in a skillet over medium heat, skin-side down, until browned. Alternately, pick the meat from the bones and use it in a pasta sauce, duck fried rice, duck tacos, or as a topping for polenta. It's also delicious in salads with bitter greens, such as endive, radicchio, arugula, or cabbage. If you remove the skin, save it to make cracklins.

Many Allium Pasta
4 servings

2 tablespoons plus 3 tablespoons extra-virgin olive oil, divided

½ cup panko bread crumbs

Kosher salt; freshly ground pepper

1 lemon

About 1½ pounds mixed alliums, such as leeks, green garlic, spring onions, sweet onions, and/or shallots

5 garlic cloves

3 tablespoons butter

Palmful of crushed red pepper flakes

1 pound spaghetti

About 1 cup freshly grated Parmigiano, plus more for the table

Anchovy fillets, for serving

Place a medium saucepan over medium heat. Add 2 tablespoons oil, then the panko. Season with salt. Toast the crumbs, tossing constantly, until golden brown and crisp, a few minutes. Scrape the crumbs onto a plate. Finely grate the zest of the lemon over and season with pepper. Toss and let cool. Wipe out the pan.

Bring a large pot of generously salted water to boil for the spaghetti. Trim and thinly slice the alliums and garlic. Cut the lemon in half, then cut one half into 4 wedges.

Heat the butter and remaining 3 tablespoons oil in the saucepan over medium-high. When the butter is foaming (don't let it brown), add the alliums. Season with salt, pepper, and pepper flakes and cook, stirring, until the vegetables soften, about 5 minutes.

Reduce the heat to medium, cover the pot, and cook, stirring every couple of minutes, until the alliums are very soft but there's still plenty of juiciness in the pot—a little texture in the onions is okay. This should take about 15 minutes; reduce the heat if needed. The beauty of this dish is that you can go as far as you want with the allium cookery. A browned onion won't be as juicy, in which case, add some water to the mixture, or reserve a little extra pasta water for adjusting the sauce. Taste and tweak as needed.

Cook the spaghetti until very al dente (2 or 3 minutes less than package instructions). Reserve 2 cups pasta water, then drain the spaghetti and return it to the pot. Add the allium sauce along with about 1 cup of pasta water. Squeeze in the juice from the lemon half. Cook over medium, tossing and stirring with tongs, until the sauce is evenly distributed and the pasta is al dente. Gradually add 1 cup Parm, tossing and adding pasta water until the noodles are generously coated.

Serve topped with bread crumbs, with lemon wedges, anchovies, and Parm to add at the table.

Coconut Chipotle Chicken
4 to 6 servings

8 bone-in, skin-on chicken thighs (about 2½ pounds total)

Kosher salt

Vegetable oil, for drizzling

2 medium yellow onions

6 garlic cloves

1 teaspoon coriander seeds, crushed

2 teaspoons mushroom powder

Large pinch of cayenne pepper

¼ cup apple cider vinegar

½ cup chipotle in adobo

2 (15-ounce) cans unsweetened coconut milk

Lime wedges, avocado, sour cream, and/or totopos, for serving

Preheat a large deep sauté pan with a lid or a Dutch oven over medium and use that time to season the chicken on the skin side with salt. Add a healthy drizzle of oil to the pan and raise the heat to medium-high. Add the chicken, skin-side down, and season the flesh side with salt. Cook, undisturbed, until the underside is crisp and almond-brown, about 15 minutes.

Turn to lightly brown the flesh side, about 3 minutes. Transfer to a rimmed baking sheet or platter. It hurts me to say this, but just in case: Reserve the drippings! (We love fat in this house and I hope also in yours.)

During chicken-browning time, finely chop or coarsely grate the onions. Roughly chop the garlic. Once the chicken has been relocated, lower the heat to medium, add the onions and garlic to the chicken fat, and season with salt. Cook, stirring, and using the liquid that the onions release to deglaze the pan, until the onion mixture is browned and softened, 8 minutes or so. Cover and cook until the garlic and onions are very smushy, about 10 minutes (check occasionally and add a splash of water if they are in any danger of drying out or scorching).

Add the coriander seeds, mushroom powder, and cayenne and cook for a couple of minutes to bloom the spices. Pour in the vinegar and raise the heat to bring to a boil. Cook, stirring occasionally, until the pan is dry. Add the chipotle and stir to coat, then pour in the coconut milk. Bring to a boil, then lower the heat to a simmer, give the liquid a taste, and adjust with salt and/or more cayenne, as needed.

Nestle the chicken thighs back into the pot, cover, and gently simmer until the chicken slides right off the bone, about 45 minutes.

Turn off the heat and let everything relax for a few. Transfer the chicken to a clean baking sheet or platter and spoon off the fat that is pooling on the surface of the sauce.

At this point, you have choices. If making ahead, you can transfer the chicken, still on the bone, to a container, and pour the braising liquid over. Let cool, then cover and chill. Or pull the meat and skin off the bones before storing. This will hold in the fridge for several days.

Alternatively, you could serve the chicken on the bone with several big spoonfuls of sauce and any of the toppings suggested for serving. Or shred the chicken, discarding the skin and bones, and serve it with the braising liquid and toppings. Or puree the sauce (without the chicken) until creamy, return it to the skillet, and warm the chicken in the sauce, either on or off the bone. It really depends how rustic or refined you want it to be when serving.

Restaurant Haze

Restaurant work began for me in 1998, at Montrachet, a three-star restaurant in Tribeca run by a tall French chef who seemed proportionally oversized for the short and narrow kitchen.

I arrived as a twenty-six-year-old culinary student, a baby whale, ready to inhale every scrap of instruction that came my way. I wasn't passive: I wanted to contribute, earn approval, and, most of all, I wanted to fit in. I was there for about a year. When I left, it was with a fledgling cook's swagger and skills that are foundational to the way I prepare food, almost thirty years later.

I was "hired" as an unpaid intern while still in culinary school and went to Montrachet straight from class. After I changed, I'd set up my workstation right on the other side of the swinging kitchen door, between a janky toaster oven and the stainless countertop where the salad cook whisked vinaigrettes in massive metal bowls. It was good that I was small. My body slid into a spot that was barely wide enough for a slim kitchen trashcan, and I could stand comfortably beneath an open shelving unit without having to crouch. I can remember feeling my hip bones press into the lip of the counter as I worked, but I can barely conjure the posh dining room. When I passed through it, I kept my eyes lowered on the red carpet and moved quickly. The kitchen staff were meant to be invisible to the guests.

In addition to helping the cooks with menial prep work—trimming vegetables, mostly—I was tasked with the amuse-bouche. This was a little bite from the chef that went out to each guest after they were seated, which meant I'd have to keep up with service, too. On my first day, Chef gave me a container of gently roasted mini sweet bell peppers and a large metal pan of cold braised rabbit. My job was to debone the rabbit and tear the meat into pieces that would fit into the cavity of each pepper.

The most efficient way to do this was by hand, digging the pieces of rabbit out of the gelatinized braising liquid, then sliding the meat off the tiny bunny bones. Once I had separated the usable bits from the discard, I would coax a pinch of shredded rabbit into the pepper, being careful not to tear the silky, floppy skin. I hadn't been at it long when the chef swooped

in behind me and said, in a searingly derisive tone: *Do you know there are oils and bacteria on your hands that you are putting into that entire batch of rabbit, causing it to become contaminated and spoil, and we will have to throw it into the garbage?* This was his way of telling me to wear gloves. Enveloped in shame and embarrassment, I knew enough to say, *Yes, Chef.* Heart pounding, I washed my hands, put on gloves, and continued with my task.

An hour later, dinner service began and orders rolled in. I stood silent and rapt, watching the cooks call back orders and fire their dishes. As though automated, they grabbed skillets and dropped them onto already-lit burners, spooned into their mise en place, squirted oil, lemon juice, and vinegar from squeeze bottles, slid aluminum trays in and out of the eye-level broiler, and monitored multiple types of proteins at once. Heeding internal timers, they bent to extract fish fillets and chicken legs from the blasting oven, then used their heels to swing the door closed behind them. My adrenaline soared.

The dance would slow when it was time to plate. From the opposite side of the counter, the chef would bend forward to scrutinize each dish being presented to him. If all went well, he'd dip a tightly rolled white napkin in a bowl of diluted white vinegar and use that to wipe the plate rim. The food runners lined up behind him, listening for him to call table numbers and positions before gliding out to the dining room with the hot plates.

The loop was closed when the runners returned with empty china, pausing in front of the chef so he could see how much (or how little) had been consumed. From there, dishes and silverware landed noisily at the dishwashing station. The porters transformed them into stacks of clean plates that made their way back to the cooks' warming shelf. I was electrified. The dining room was pomp, performance, a show. The kitchen was unedited, raw sport, a coordinated mosh pit. It seemed like the most beautiful transaction imaginable. The diners order the food, we cook the food, they eat the food, we wash the dishes, they give us money, they leave, we leave.

I made sure to be on time, take up a minimum of space, heed the chef, help the cooks, and keep up with the *amuse*. Soon, I was offered an actual staff position: $350 for a six-day week; we worked a double on Fridays and the restaurant was closed on Sundays. No sick days, no vacation. It was a low wage for the overtime hours and the nonexistent benefits. But it was a line position. I'd be an entremetier, preparing the vegetables that went with the fish entrées. I accepted on the spot. The shitty pay and punishing conditions were, unfortunately, a big part of the draw, my chance to rebel against my privileged upbringing and fancy education. I wanted to be tough; I wanted to be a player in the behind-the-scenes ruckus of it, anonymous to the diners but indispensable to the team. There was something so sexy to me about being a woman in this masculine space, where I'd get dirty and sweaty flinging skillets all night. I had no idea what I was doing, but I desperately needed to prove I could do it. To them, and to myself.

At Montrachet, cooking went from a hobby to grueling work that destroyed any desire I had to cook on my days off. Or, day: Sunday. I arrived for my shift in a state of panic, which ebbed and peaked depending on factors out of my control—how many reservations were on the books, when food deliveries arrived, the amount of prep on the to-do list, Chef's mood.

I reported to the fish cook, Max, a six-foot-tall, effortlessly cool woman with spiky, platinum hair; long, graceful fingers; and several years of kitchen experience. She intimidated me, I needed to please her, I was a little bit in love with her, and I wanted to be her. She was mysterious, humorless, and unflappable. Hot. Most of the time, I assumed she wanted to throttle me, which felt warranted given my naiveté. Fucking something up and wasting product was my main fear; as was falling behind during service. Like being sucked into a tornado, you have time to recognize your demise coming, but not enough to avoid it. No matter what was happening, I actively tried not to anger or annoy Max.

The hierarchy of a French kitchen is based on a battle brigade, and that kitchen was assigned macho at birth. My performance anxiety was coupled with the culture shock of existing in an overwhelmingly masculine environment. I expected to be ogled and I was waiting to be belittled. There was no escaping my femaleness, yet femininity had no role in the group dynamic. The process of shedding my girlhood started in the co-ed changing area when I disrobed alongside four men, then slid into a boxy white chef's jacket and the polyester checkered pants that were cut for a man's body. I did this as quickly as possible, staring straight into the wall. Earning respect and being less femme were entwined.

In the kitchen, I wanted to transcend "not bad for a girl." I refused to be seen as weak, and wouldn't let my male colleagues hoist heavy pots for me. Eventually they stopped offering. If something was out of reach, I didn't ask long-limbed Max to get it for me, either. She'd signaled early on that she couldn't interrupt her flow every time I needed something. Like a stubborn toddler set on doing whatever the big kids could do, I'd climb up on the stainless counters in my socked feet to fetch the tall stockpot, the steamer basket, the giant colander stored on the highest shelves. My war paint was the olive oil I'd rub on my lips when they got chapped from ducking in and out of a 500°F oven all day. I lost weight from the long days of physical labor, and Max showed me how to twist strips of plastic wrap into makeshift belts that we used to keep our pants up.

I kept up my tough-guy masquerade and assimilated to the job. I diligently followed Max's directions, leaning into the corrections she gave me, and parroted her motions when we were in service. Within a couple of months, I went from my amuse-bouche station to finding my own physical flair on the line. I could juggle multiple skillets at once. I knew when to add water to a pan of sautéed vegetables to create a blast of steam that would finish cooking them through. I liked to hook my first two fingers into the butter at my station, then whip my wrist to launch that knob of dairy into a sauté pan and swirl it to emulsify a sauce. I was good at memorizing the combination of dishes the chef fired, murmuring, *You ready?* to Max at the exact moment her branzino was cooked through, the two of us turning in unison to plate the next dish.

I wasn't excellent, but I tried really hard, and I started to feel Max soften toward me. She was always quiet and stoic during rare lulls in service, not engaging in frivolous side talk, while I wiped down our station, refilled our squeeze bottles, checked and triple-checked our backup containers. After especially long nights, she'd sometimes decide to prepare a second family meal for the cooks, and I'd help her throw together ingredients for a quick puttanesca pasta that we'd eat standing up. She told me about her fantasy of opening a super-casual fish restaurant in Northern California, with intentionally uncomfortable wooden benches for seats and a view of the coast. The concept was about as different from Montrachet as I could fathom, and it made me realize her dreams diverged radically from the predictable course we were on. She was the most punk rock, the coolest of the cool girls.

One night after work, Max invited me to get drinks at the bar on the corner, a legendary local spot that was popular with the staff. I was surprised, excited, and nervous about socializing with her, even though we were bonded at the hip for twelve hours a day, six days a week. To cope, I got absolutely shit-faced on anise-flavored Pernod and water. (Don't ask

why that old-guy aperitif was my drink at the time.) I remember realizing with embarassment that I had never changed out of my kitchen clogs, and when I accidentally knocked over a drink and sent sticky Pernod flying all over the bar, I decided to call it a night.

The next day, I woke up to the most horrific, crushing hangover of my life. Blind with nausea, head like cement blocks grinding together, and on shaky legs, I could barely stand up without gagging. The usual antidote—a bacon-egg-and-cheese with a Coke—was out of the question. I was ill and incapacitated, but I could not call out of work. There was no one to cover my shift. Certainly not on this day, because it was Saturday, and Valentine's Day, a notorious night to be a line cook. The dining room would be packed with two-tops to squeeze in as many doe-eyed couples as would fit. There was lobster on the prix fixe menu, which meant Max and I were going to get clobbered. If I didn't show, she'd have to do the two-person job alone, and all of my gains would be blown to bits.

I still snip the rubber bands first

Duty called. I walked into the kitchen late, wearing sunglasses. Max took one look at me, rolled her eyes, and went back to her cutting board. Sympathy was not on the menu. First up: We had to cook and shell about sixty lobsters. I set up opposite Max; she would cook and I would process, in an assembly line. When the first batch of lobsters had met their steamy demise, she plopped them into a long metal pan, slid it across the counter to me, and turned around to do more murder. I was expected to shell as quickly as possible.

I wanted to die, but I could not quit. I twisted the tail off of the lobster's body, releasing a fragrant gust of steaming lobster guts into my face. I immediately dropped to the floor in a crouch, with one hand pressed into the rubber kitchen mat on the floor. This seemed like a logical place to wait for the nausea to pass. When I could stand again, it was back to business.

Are you going to make it? Max asked, irritated.

Me? Oh yeah, I said, *I'm good.*

That initial lobster established the pattern I was locked into until my crustacean circle of shell was over: liberate the tail, unleash tomalley facial, succumb, stand, proceed. This, dozens of times.

When the chef walked in, he found me down on one knee, prayerful and remorseful. I heard him ask, *Is she okay?* Max replied: *Hangover.* From the floor, I chimed in: *It was Pernod.* He let out a groan. *Pernod! You were drinking Pernod?? This is the worst hangover you can ever have.* He went on and on about it, how bad Pernod hit the next day, as if I didn't know. When I stood back up he looked me in the eye and said: *Once you get on the line and start sweating, you'll be fine. You'll sweat it all out. Trust me.* I did not believe him, but when I took my place on the hot line, either the sweat cured me, or we were too buried in tickets for me to have body awareness. I made it through the night, earning some sort of battle badge, surviving a rite of passage. I didn't ditch. I faced the consequences. And I'm pretty sure I never drank Pernod again.

Working while sick was an unspoken part of the job, not only because we weren't entitled to paid sick days. There were heaps of other injustices that

I filed under Stuff That Toughens You Up. The suffering wasn't saved for me, and in fact, people who had been there longer were vulnerable to far worse.

It was a package deal. I was learning to cook for real, and I was learning what it took to be a cook. I was getting paid, which meant I would stay quiet when our chef threw a molten-hot sizzle tray straight out of the salamander at the cook standing next to me, hitting him in the chest. He would do this when, say, a duck breast was undercooked. Sometimes Chef would just berate him, viciously, for overreducing the demi-glace that went with the sweetbreads. When the chef let loose, the rest of us would stand respectfully silent. I squirmed through mixed feelings of empathy for my coworker and gratitude that I wasn't in his shoes. On more than one occasion, the captain came into the kitchen to tell the chef that his yelling was audible to the guests in the dining room. When the tantrum was over, we'd swing right back into it like nothing had happened, the kitchen noticeably more quiet afterward.

I had officially romanticized being a professional cook, the beauty and ugliness of the job balancing each other like butter and salt. Sure, the pay was shit, and no, it's not okay to normalize workplace violence. But (here comes the irrational upside), I got to touch the most beautiful ingredients I'd ever seen—wild black trumpet mushrooms delivered in shallow cardboard boxes littered with pine needles and scraps of wet leaves from where they were foraged. Dayboat sea scallops so fresh the flesh undulated when the chef cut into them, the muscle still alive. I tasted delicacies for the first time: crosnes, Tristar strawberries, sea beans, black truffles, sweetbreads.

Every night I stood elbow-to-elbow with the fish cook on one side and the meat cook on the other, watching and learning how hot a pan had to be to sear tiny Taylor Bay scallops and encase them in lemony brown butter without overcooking them. (I still make a version of this at home with sea scallops and a spicy cumin butter.) I ate chewy nubs of duck breast anchored to crisp fat off the meat cook's cutting board; we never sent out the end pieces, only the prized slices from the widest part of the breast. My obsessive brain was subdued by being consistent, nailing the cookery, getting my dishes up on time, not running out midservice.

It has taken me this long to detangle the hardness of that work from the nostalgia I feel about everything I learned. I believed that starting out in kitchens should be brutal; we were warned about it in cooking school the way actors are prepped for audition rejections. Surely if I wasn't worthy of this occupation, I'd be asked to leave. In late-90s logic, being "cut out for it" meant I could (must?) handle the hardness, too. The physically taxing and emotionally draining environment validated my world view that work *should* be tough. (Throw every eldest daughter trope at me—I will overachieve 'til I drop.) Being a line cook was outrageous and incredible. It was exploitative and thrilling. It was a job that made me both expect and tolerate bad behavior, and unfortunately I internalized that perspective and brought it to every other workplace I entered afterward, in ways that I deeply regret. But, still. I never wanted to be anyplace more.

Montrachet taught me that fear and growth are intertwined. It helped me realize I enjoy being at the bottom of a learning curve. That's made it easier for me to take risks ever since. I don't miss the people I worked with; I can't remember most of their names, except for Max, whom I've tried (and failed) to track down many times. I no longer accept that restaurant kitchens should be run like that. How to shell a lobster, though—I still do as I was shown, and have taught my sons to do it that way, too, minus the hangover. I preheat my carbon-steel skillet until it's matte and near-molten to get the most glorious sear on my scallops. I can flip food in a skillet with my left hand while salt cascades from the fingers of my right, and I know how to get fish fillets to lie flat in the pan from watching Max do it over and over, all night long. It was many years before cooking at home was fun for me again, and I never want that feeling to go away. If I overcook a steak, I don't throw hot plates. We eat it anyway, of course, with some spicy mayo to camouflage the error.

Montrachet is gone now, as is the bar on the corner (it closed and then reopened as a J.Crew, which was sad). The stinky phone booth where I used to call my husband-to-be after work doesn't exist, either. Uber drivers don't argue with me about going over the bridge to Brooklyn, like cabbies sometimes did when I'd splurge on a taxi home. I don't have a single photograph from that time. In a way, I'm glad, because everything that happened there can stay exactly how I remember it. When I'm on that block in Tribeca now, I have to search to find any familiar landmarks from when I walked out of the restaurant. But if I close my eyes, it rolls like a movie. It's hard to fathom that young woman was me, diving into a world of cooking that would become her entire life. It wasn't a dream. The adrenaline that hit me that first night of service was a thunderbolt of pure love that I still feel for the job I chose. I'm grateful the hardness is mostly gone, and not a bit sorry for finding out who I am.

Seared Scallops with Chile-Cumin Butter
Serves 2

1 teaspoon Aleppo pepper

½ teaspoon cumin seeds, crushed

Pinch of sugar

½ pound large dry-packed scallops

Kosher salt

Vegetable oil

Cooked white rice, for serving

2 tablespoons butter

Unseasoned rice vinegar

Chile oil (optional)

Preheat a heavy skillet over medium for 5 minutes. In a small bowl, mix the Aleppo, cumin, and sugar. Pat the scallops dry and season them with salt.

Add enough oil to lightly and evenly coat the pan. Increase the heat to medium-high and place the scallops on one of their flat sides, pressing lightly with your fingers or the round side of a spoon so that they press against the surface. Cook, without bothering them, until they are chestnut brown on the underside, 3 to 5 minutes.

Turn the scallops over—preferably by lifting them up and nudging them over with a sauce spoon, which could look and feel nonchalant and edgy, like purposely tapping ash from a cigarette. Just make sure they end up on the other flat side. Continue to cook until barely cooked through—a slightly translucent beltline is okay—30 seconds longer. Divide the scallops among bowls of rice. Turn off the heat under the skillet.

Add the butter and the spices to the skillet. There should be enough residual heat to melt the butter completely. Turn the heat to low and lightly brown the butter, toasting the spices in the process, and stirring frequently, 3 to 4 minutes. Stop the cooking with a spoonful of vinegar, then stir and swirl the pan to bring the sauce together. If it's overreduced and looks greasy, loosen it up with a spoonful of water, then cook, stirring, until it emulsifies. Taste the sauce for salt.

Spoon the spiced butter over the scallops and rice. If desired, drizzle with some chile oil.

PERNOD
45

Lobster Max's Way, with Spicy Mayo
For 2

- ½ cup mayonnaise
- 2 teaspoons fresh lime juice (from 1 lime)
- 2 teaspoons sambal oelek or Sriracha
- 1 teaspoon fish sauce
- Kosher salt
- 2 whole live lobsters (1¼ to 1½ pounds each)
- Lemon wedges and flaky salt, for serving

In a small bowl, stir together the mayo, lime juice, sambal, and fish sauce. Taste and season with a pinch of salt and/or more fish sauce. Refrigerate the spicy mayo while you steam the lobsters.

Bring several inches of generously seasoned water to a boil in a tall stockpot or large Dutch oven over high heat. Snip the rubber bands off the lobsters' claws. In culinary school, they taught us to kill the lobster quickly by bisecting its head straight down the middle with a chef's knife before steaming it, but none of the restaurants I worked for subsequently did that, so neither do I.

Swiftly place the lobsters in the pot and cover it with the lid (they don't need to be submerged). Reduce the heat to medium-high and cook the lobsters until the shells are bright red and the thickest part of the tail meat is cooked through, 12 to 14 minutes. (If you have a digital thermometer, stick it into the center of the top segment of the tail; the temperature should register 140°F.)

Transfer the lobsters to a rimmed baking sheet and let sit for a couple of minutes. Working with one lobster at a time, wrap the tail in a kitchen towel and twist the tail until it comes free, then twist off the claws where they attach to the body. Twist the legs off the claws (the part often referred to as the "knuckles") and set them aside.

Pull down on the thumb of the claw until you hear it pop and release (liquid will pour out of the base of the claw, so do this over the baking sheet or the sink). Tease and wiggle the thumb shell off the rest of the claw. There may be a flat piece of cartilage inside the meaty part of the claw, which you can deal with when you eat it.

Next, place the claws on a cutting board with the kitchen towel wrapped around them. Give a few whacks with the blunt side of a heavy knife or a meat mallet until you feel the shell crack apart. Try not to obliterate the shell, which will in turn flatten and shred the meat.

I would serve each lobster on a plate with lemon wedges and flaky salt in these five pieces—tail, legs, and cracked claws—and let each person finish shelling them at the table (see Eating with Your Hands, page 70). Divide the mayo between two bowls and arm yourselves with a clean kitchen towel in addition to a napkin. Put out an empty bowl for the shells.

To remove the tail meat, drape a kitchen towel over the tail and grip it with both hands like you're holding a steering wheel, hump up. Squeeze the tail inward with your hands until you feel the tail crack along its length. Flip it over so it's belly-side up and bend the outer edges of the shell back to split it open. (You can also cut the shell open with kitchen shears.) Remove the tail meat. Cut it into pieces and dip into the mayo as you go.

Because the claws are precracked, each person should have no trouble getting into the meat, but if you have lobster crackers, they can be helpful. Eat the claw meat dipped in mayo. Use shears to cut the knuckles open to get into the little nuggets of meat inside.

You should make the long, thin walking legs that extend from the top part of the lobster's body available to your guest. Some people like to nibble and suck on them, and who are we to get in the way of that?

Crispy-Skinned Fish with Olives and Lemon
4 servings

3 lemons

8 Castelvetrano olives, preferably with pits

1 small shallot

4 skin-on branzino or red snapper fillets (6 to 8 ounces each)

Kosher salt

Vegetable oil

4 tablespoons (2 ounces/ ½ stick) unsalted butter, cut into 4 pieces

Cut 2 lemons in half and squeeze them to yield ¼ cup juice. You might not need both lemons, but you never know. Cut 8 thin rounds from the remaining lemon. Set the juice and lemon rounds aside. Smash the olives to remove the pits, then tear the flesh into small pieces. Set olives aside. Mince the shallot and—you guessed it—set aside.

Heat a heavy 12-inch stainless-steel skillet over medium heat for 3 to 5 minutes. While you wait, season both sides of the fillets with salt.

If your largest skillet won't accommodate all of the fish fillets at the same time, do this next step in two batches. Increase the heat to medium-high and drizzle a small amount of oil into the pan, tilt to coat, then quickly (and carefully) wipe out the pan with paper towel. Preheating and greasing the pan will make it virtually nonstick.

Return the skillet to the heat and add enough oil to evenly coat the surface without any bald spots. Carefully lower the fish into the pan, skin-side down. As soon as they curl up and buckle, something all proteins do when they hit high heat, tilt the pan to let oil run underneath the fillets, then use a slotted fish spatula to gently press the flesh flat against the pan.

Cook, lightly pressing down occasionally, until the skin is golden brown and crisp and the fillet is mostly cooked through, with a rare strip down the center, 2 to 3 minutes. Carefully turn fish over and cook until just cooked through, about 2 minutes more.

Transfer the fillets to serving plates while you make the sauce. Quickly rinse out the pan, then wipe it dry. Return to medium heat and add the butter. When the foaming subsides and the butter is starting to brown, add the shallot and lemon slices. Cook, stirring gently, until the shallot is translucent and the lemon is softened, about 2 minutes.

Add 3 tablespoons lemon juice, the olive pieces, and a splash of water. Cook, swirling the pan to emulsify the sauce. Taste the sauce and adjust seasoning with salt and more lemon juice, if needed. Remove from the heat and stir in the chives.

Spoon the pan sauce to the side of the fish to serve.

Eat Like a Child

My first word was "cookie." When I said it, my parents would give me a cookie—we were communicating! According to legend, I was soon demanding cookies nonstop.

For me, eating like a child doesn't conjure chicken fingers from the kids' menu. Rather, it's the act of eating free of inhibitions. It's the way both of my babies nursed, held against my body, rhythmically drinking until the fatty hindmilk hit them. Then, they'd slow. I'd gaze down at them as they slept on a giant boob, milk-drunk and slack-mouthed. Sustenance and pleasure, hard-wired from the start.

I think of the way baby Leo's eyes widened after my sister deposited a dollop of whipped cream on his mouth before he'd ever had a taste of solid food, and how his hand shot out to grab more. I remember finding toddler Cosmo crouched behind a living room chair with his Easter basket, coated in chocolate from his hairline to his wrists. I think of the pictures I have of Cosmo, seated at a table, a bowl tipped to his face to get the last licks of whatever was in there (ice cream, usually), and the fistfuls of vanilla-scented pancakes he would drown in maple syrup. There's the memory of six-year-old Leo's look of wonderment when I showed him how to straighten the bottom corner of a bag of Doritos to trash-chute the salty fragments into his mouth.

Leo, on a table, with a banana

One Friday during the summer after the separation, Cosmo and I drove upstate to spend the weekend with my parents. As usual, I was running late, and in my underfed and traffic-is-worsening panic, I asked Cosmo to make us peanut butter and jelly sandwiches for the road. He ate his in the car, but by then the appetite-suppressing effects of my iced coffee had kicked in, and I'd realized how impossible it would be to eat a PB&J and drive at the same time.

After we arrived, I unwrapped the sandwich and was hit by its sculptural artistry and its genius. The bread was cut unevenly, super thick on one side of the slices and razor-thin on the other, allowing the jam to soak through the crumb and smear all over the plastic wrap. There was an amount of peanut butter I would never have had the guts to use; it was

half the sandwich, by height. The jam was spread like mortar in equal proportion. His entire personality was all over the architecture of this sandwich: unrestrained.

At first I thought, *I can't eat this whole thing.* It was huge—it was too much. But Cosmo hadn't cut it in half before wrapping it, so I had no choice but to approach it, whole, from an outside corner. Once I started, there was no natural place to stop. Consuming it was astounding and messy. As I made my way toward the center, the edges of the bread brushed up against my cheeks, sticking to my humidity-frizzed hair. Cosmo hadn't spread the peanut butter to the edges of the crusts. I tore them free and used them as shovels to scoop out (and eat) the jam from the thickest part. Who makes a sandwich like this?? Well, Cosmo does, and it mirrored his spirit: unconcerned with rules, infinitely confident, insatiable. Finishing the PB&J was like being rolled in whitewater. Let it happen. There, in my parents' house, I ate my remarkable child's sandwich like I was still a child myself. I remembered how fantastic it is to eat someone else's food, trusting that whatever is being offered is going to be good.

There is never "too much of a good thing." There are too many bad things. Way too many. If you can experience fleeting joy in a PB&J, a fat pat of butter, a bowl of melting ice cream, wrap yourself in it.

The triumphant sandwich Cosmo made for me

Cosmo's PB&PB&J&J&J
Makes 1 Crazy Sandwich

As told by Cosmo Music

Loaf of sandwich bread

Peanut butter, preferably crunchy

Honey, for drizzling

Flaky salt

Jam, preferably raspberry

Before you start, set your intentions. The number one setback when making a sandwich for someone else is the fear that there's too much sandwich, which is nonsense. You want your sandwich to be 100 percent sandwich. That goes for all food.

Cut 2 slices of bread, thicker than you've been taught. Exceed expectations.

There are two ways you can go from here: One is toasting said bread, and the other is—if you didn't already guess—not toasting said bread. I prefer the not-toasting, as it allows the bread to soak up the peanut butter/jelly mixture better.

Spread the peanut butter onto one piece of bread, generously. Don't hold back. Drizzle freely with honey, which is more fun if you do it from a great height. Season with flaky salt. Spackle the other slice of bread with a generous layer of jam. Be free. Close up the sandwich and wrap in wax paper. This sandwich is best if left to age for an hour or two at room temperature, during which time the ingredients will become one with one another.

Extremely Floofy Vanilla Pancakes

Makes twelve to sixteen 3-inch pancakes; recipe is easily doubled

2 cups (240g) all-purpose flour

2 teaspoons baking soda

1½ teaspoons baking powder

2 tablespoons sugar, divided

1 teaspoon kosher salt, plus a pinch

2 cups buttermilk

2 large eggs

1½ teaspoons vanilla extract

4 tablespoons (57g; ½ stick) unsalted butter, melted

Vegetable oil, ghee, coconut oil, or shortening, for the griddle

Maple syrup or whatever you like on your pancakes

Heat a griddle to 375°F or place your largest cast-iron or stainless-steel skillet over medium- to medium-high while you make the batter.

In a large bowl, whisk together the flour, baking soda, baking powder, 1 tablespoon sugar, and 1 teaspoon salt. This will end up being the bowl for the batter, so give yourself a little room.

Pour the buttermilk into a measuring cup. Crack the eggs into a clean, medium bowl, being careful not to break the yolks. With your fingers, gently pick up the yolks one at a time and drop them into the buttermilk. (Just lift them up and let the whites dangle back down.) Whisk the egg whites until frothy, then add a pinch of salt and whisk until the whites are barely opaque and starting to form very floppy ridges. Gradually whisk in the remaining 1 tablespoon sugar and keep going until the whites are shiny and hold a wobbly, just-firm peak.

Add the vanilla to the buttermilk and whisk to break up the yolks. Pour the buttermilk mixture into the dry ingredients, then drizzle the melted butter over. Gently fold with a rubber spatula until the batter is pretty chunky and lumpy, but there's no dry flour in the bottom of the bowl, 5 or 6 folds. Gently fold in the egg whites—err on the side of undermixing; a few streaks of whites and some lumps make for loftier pancakes.

Generously grease the hot griddle with your fat of choice. Spoon the batter onto the skillet in roughly ⅓-cup amounts—it's so annoying to dole the batter out like this, so do it to get a visual on the first couple and then switch to a large spoon. Feel free to make bigger or smaller pancakes, too! My timing is based on roughly 3 ounces of batter, though. Just know that.

Cook until lazy bubbles appear in the center of the pancakes, about 2 minutes. Gently turn—you should see them puff and rise when the uncooked side comes in contact with the hot griddle. Cook until the second side is richly browned, about 3 minutes more.

Some tips: If you want a raised, crispy edge on the top side of your pancakes, add more grease to the griddle. If the pancakes are coming out with a sort of matte, flat, evenly colored top side, it's fine, but it's because you skimped on the fat. If the pancakes overcook, they'll start to deflate. If they're undercooked, the interior will be slightly gummy. Work it out with your stove and the heat level that gets you closest to this timing. You know what they say about the first pancake. You might need to tinker a bit.

At my house, these pancakes come with butter and maple syrup. But if I was at your house and you put them out with sugar and raspberry jam, I'd be psyched. The one thing I never want, though, is a hot blueberry, so please don't put them in the batter.

The Hardest Way Is Chef's Way

About two years after leaving my job at Montrachet, after a stint as a private chef, I was hired as a line cook at Union Pacific, near the Flatiron building in Manhattan.

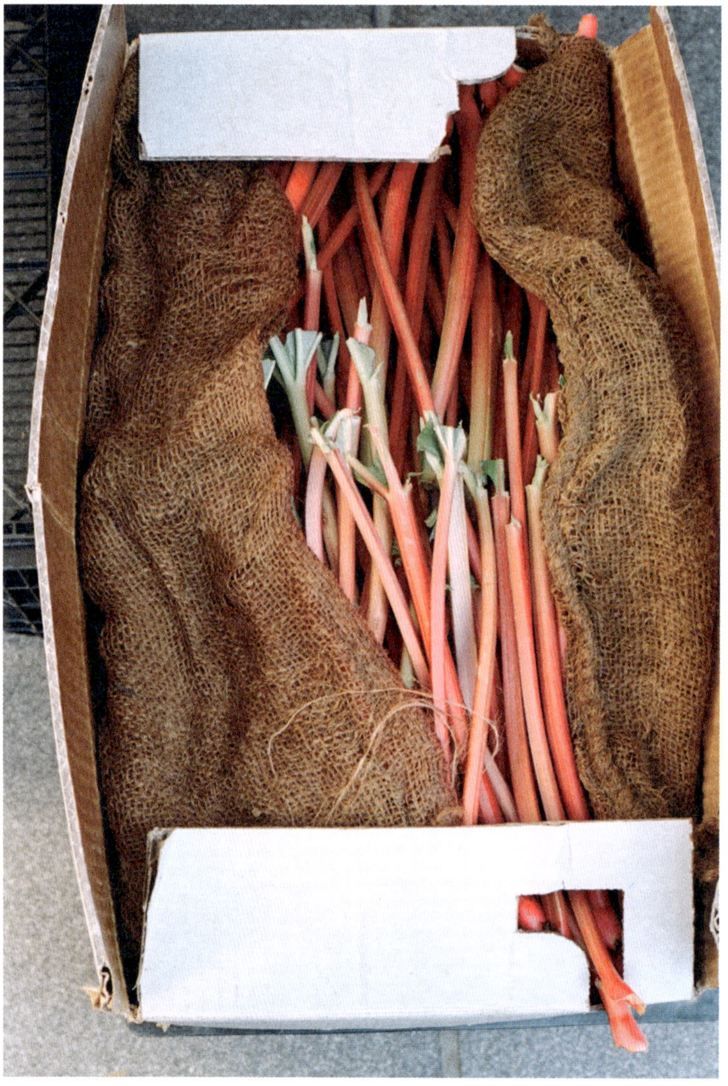

The actual favas I worked less hard on

Famed *New York Times* restaurant reviewer Ruth Reichl had awarded chef Rocco DiSpirito three stars for his menu there, a chic melding of French techniques with ingredients from other cuisines—Japanese, Vietnamese, and Indian in particular. Braised short ribs with truffled taro root; raw scallops and uni; a rhubarb and rice vinegar compote sweetened with burnt caramel. At the time, these pairings were cutting-edge. I was the meat entremetier, and the dishes were much more complex than at Montrachet, with multiple subrecipes required to plate a single item. It was also the first place I worked that had sous-chefs—three men—all graduates of the "you're an idiot" school of motivation.

One of those sous-chefs said four things of great consequence to me. My favorite was *Beat it, douchebag,* which he would blurt into my ear as he knocked into me on his way to somewhere else. The first time he said it, I was concurrently shocked and attracted to the audacity. I love cursing, and I appreciated the pointedness of the message. I hadn't used "douchebag" as an insult since high school—cute. It was effective, but not because it got me out of his way. He told me to move *as* he pushed past; the shoulder check was gratuitous. It was an announcement that he had arrived for work and wanted me to be aware of his physical presence. That's how you make people shrink.

Then there was the Very Worst Day of Being a Line Cook Ever. I was late for my Saturday shift, and there was no way in hell I was going to finish making onion soubise in time for service. When I threw several pounds of butter into a hot rondeau, and started maniacally slicing white onions, the meat cook—my station partner—shook his head sadly and said, *You're starting that now?* Then he went back to his own prep.

His reaction was tame compared to what came later. I was supposed to cook the onions with turmeric slowly for hours, until the onions melted into the spiced butter, creating a vibrant sauce. Instead, the soubise was still

on the stove when the first tickets were fired at 5:30 p.m. The mixture was greasy instead of emulsified, the onions crunchy, the turmeric unpleasantly pungent and dusty-tasting. It was all I had. When I sent the first portion to the service pass, douchebag sous-chef took one taste, dropped his spoon onto his cutting board, and turned around dramatically slowly, eventually making eye contact with me.

That's the most disgusting thing I've ever put in my mouth, he said.

Yes, Chef.

A different day, I was in the basement prep kitchen, where menial tasks took place in the hours leading up to dinner service: trimming and peeling mountains of vegetables, cutting rigid sweet potatoes and celery root into neat, eighth-inch cubes, reducing gallons of stock and wine for demi-glace. The mood down there was less busy bee, more panicked horse. The race toward service quashed any banter among the cooks. I was at the deep, three-bay sink area, filling and emptying the basins with water to wash case after case of mature spinach until no grit remained. Each batch had to be submerged and swished at least three times; the water was so cold it made my hands ache and itch. The possibility that a diner might bite down on sandy spinach and send the dish back was a horror I didn't think I'd survive. Simultaneously monotonous and high-stakes. The sous-chef stopped to fill up a quart container of water where I was working, and I took that opportunity to groan and tell him that I hated washing spinach.

Dead eyes: *Why?* Wasn't it obvious?

Because it takes so fucking long.

He looked me up and down, clocking the moron standing in front of him.

Then do it faster.

My kids like this story, but they hate it when I say that to them.

My next lesson came in spring, while I was shelling and blanching fava beans, a fleeting crop that we were showcasing on a pretty pasta and in a shaved artichoke salad. I'd been taught to remove the individual beans from their thick, fuzzy outer pod, then peel off the light green skin that tightly encased each prized bean inside. Then I'd cook the beans in boiling salted water just long enough to barely soften them—30 seconds—and immediately plunge them into an ice bath to set their shamrock-green color. Picking the skin off was laborious, and rushing made it too easy to break a bean, which were prettiest on the plate when they were intact.

By then, I knew better than to complain. I adopted the tone of a curious student consulting her wise tutor when I asked douchebag, do-it-faster sous-chef why we peeled the favas raw, instead of cooking them in the skin and *then* peeling them. (Blanching softens the skin and the bean pops right out, but of course he already knew that.)

He responded: *Peeling them first is harder, and if Chef has a choice between the hard way or the easy way, he's always going to choose harder, because it's probably better. That's why.*

I nodded. In distorted kitchen culture, his reasoning made perfect sense: Irrational suffering guarantees quality.

I thought about this twenty-two years later, solo in the separation sublet one weekend in June. I had gotten a heap of young garlic, spring onions, and favas from the farmers' market with no recipe in mind. (When green things return to the market, my rule is buy first, make decisions later.) It was only a month or so since the split, but cooking for myself was already a trusted time-passing technique.

A simple spring pasta started to take shape. I put on a pot of water for blanching the beans and cooking the noodles. While it heated, I liberated the individual fava beans from their long pods. I had a decision to make. Peel, then blanch? Or blanch, then peel? One was harder and possibly better. The other was easier and—what? Worse? Or simply not the way I'd been instructed? With the benefit of a lifetime of fava bean cookery behind me, I asked myself: *Why do we do this the hard way? Because an infallible chef decided it was more interesting if his staff had to struggle?* Well, that was a ridiculous answer.

I was a handful of favas in when I gave myself permission to stop doing it the hard way. *I'm the boss of me now,* I said to the cutting board, *and picking the skin off these beans is a level of suffering I am no longer willing to engage in.* So there!

I tolerated Union Pacific's toughness by choice, as a younger person seeking marketable skills and experience. I accepted that these teachings would be hammered into me by people I respected for being the better cooks. That they were also at ease physically intimidating me was harder to parse. The present notion that I could wrest hardship from worthiness felt radical, but it was also as simple as whether I peeled a bean or not. It shows how much I was in my head to admit this, but I'm serious: the fava was a metaphor for my life. Here goes: The decision to get divorced was brutal; the only reason I was putting myself through it was because I believed it would lead to future happiness. What could I gain from subjecting myself to fava-related injustices? The echoes of a bully's words to me? Madness! I would blanch, and then peel, those goddamn fava beans, because they were already good, and I had nothing to prove to anyone.

I was cooking for one and the prep work went quickly. The parboiled favas slid right out of their pale green pouches—as I knew they would—aided by a thin slick of cooking liquid. I sizzled the onions and young garlic in lots of olive oil, seasoned with salt, black pepper, and a pinch of red pepper flakes—the tried-and-true aglio e olio treatment. When the pasta was ready—medium shells that would harbor beans inside their cavities—I scooped it into the pan with the onions and added the favas, then tossed it together with pasta water and Parm. I topped my bowlful with shavings of ricotta salata and enjoyed the seasonal special while it was still light out.

My techniques were smart; the dish looked beautiful, I loved eating it, and it was fast, too. If you were to ask me, that's the way it should be done.

Burnt Caramel Rhubarb Compote
Makes 1½ cups

½ cup sugar, plus more if needed

¼ cup unseasoned rice vinegar, plus more if needed

1 pound rhubarb (about 6 medium stalks), cut into 2-inch lengths

Kosher salt

Make a dry caramel: Place ½ cup sugar in a medium saucepan set over medium heat. Cook, without stirring, until the sugar begins to liquefy around the edges, 3 or 4 minutes. Cook, periodically using a spoon to drag the melted edge of the sugar toward the center, until all of the sugar has melted, about 3 minutes more.

Continue cooking, swirling the pan rather than stirring, until the caramel is a deep amber color and wisps of smoke are visible, about 3 minutes longer. It's better to err on the slow side while doing this, so if it takes a little longer than indicated, be patient rather than cranking the heat.

Remove the saucepan from the heat and carefully, but swiftly, pour in the vinegar. The mixture will bubble up violently and then seize. Add the rhubarb and a big pinch of salt and return to medium heat. Stir to coat the rhubarb in the caramel. It will be thick and very sticky at first, but will thin out as the rhubarb releases juice. Cook, stirring occasionally, until the mixture comes to a simmer, about 4 minutes.

Partially cover and cook the compote over medium-low heat until the rhubarb has collapsed into shreds, about 10 minutes. Simmer, uncovered, until the compote has thickened slightly and the liquid is syrupy, another 5 to 7 minutes. Transfer to a bowl to cool.

Once it's cool enough to taste, assess the balance of sweet and sour in the mixture. If it's too tart, stir in some sugar until dissolved and taste again. If it is overly sweet, adjust with more vinegar and/or salt. I like it stirred into plain yogurt, but it's also a tasty condiment for savory things, like Duck Confit (page 112).

Justice-for-Favas Spring Pasta
Serves 2

2 pounds fresh fava beans, in the pod

¼ cup extra-virgin olive oil, plus more for drizzling

1 small head green garlic, or 4 large garlic cloves, thinly sliced

1 small shallot, thinly sliced

2 spring (bulb) onions, white and light-green parts only, thinly sliced

Kosher salt; freshly ground pepper

8 ounces large pasta shells

¼-pound wedge ricotta salata

Parmigiano, for serving

Bring a large pot of generously salted water to a boil.

Remove the fava beans from their pods. Blanch the beans in the boiling water just to soften them, about 30 seconds, then remove them with a mesh strainer and rinse under cold water until cool enough to handle. (Save the pot of water; you'll use it to cook the pasta.) Pinch an edge of the skin open with your fingertips, then push out the bean. You should have a heaping cup of beans. Discard the skins.

Combine the oil and garlic in a large saucepan over medium-low heat. Cook, stirring, until you see some sizzling, about 5 minutes.

Add the shallot and spring onions. Season with salt and pepper. Cook until the onions are floppy, a few minutes. Reduce the heat to low, cover the pan, and cook until everything is silky and golden, about 5 minutes more. Remove from the heat.

Bring the water back to a boil and cook the pasta until very al dente, 3 minutes less than the package indicates. Use a spider to transfer the pasta to the allium mixture (alternately, reserve about a cup of pasta water, then drain the pasta and add it to the allium mixture). Add the favas and about ½ cup pasta water to the pasta and vegetables along with a glug of oil. Cook, tossing and stirring over medium heat and adding additional pasta water as needed, until the pasta is al dente and suspended in a glossy, slightly thickened sauce, 3 or 4 minutes. Check for seasoning and adjust as needed.

Divide the pasta between bowls and use a vegetable peeler to shave ricotta salata on top. Pass the Parm at the table.

4.
Mother Sauce

TOASTED COCONUT
CHEMICAL BANK
ASK US ABOUT NO FEE
NY
ATM: 69-1
FDHS
This Identifies: No 638
Carla Lalli
as a passenger of the Liberty Lines
Express, Inc. for the School
FDHS
This Identifies: No 927
Carla Lalli
as a passenger of the Liberty Lines
Express, Inc. for the School Year
1988. This pass is valid ONLY
designated School Routes
1988
Terminating: June 30, 1988
I love you
Providence,

CLM

Mother Sauce

When I was ten or eleven, there was nothing better than being asked what I wanted for dinner on Saturday night. The answer was Alfredo, and my mom was always willing to make it.

I remember sitting at the dinner table while my mom stood at the range and cooked, her back turned to the kitchen. My sister, Nina, was perched in her highchair. My parents ate after we did—at 9 p.m. or later—an entirely different meal my mom would prepare.

Alfredo is a one-pot dish. She'd stir the sauce together in the same pot she'd used to boil the pasta. Her Alfredo had three ingredients: unsalted butter, grated Parmigiano, and pasta water. No cream, no milk, no flour. She made it without measurements, adding splashes of pasta water and however much butter was needed to give her palmfuls of Parm something to melt into. It was pale-yellow, glossy, and almost sticky when it was done, nothing like the thick, milky pool of sauce I'd encounter when I went to Olive Garden with my grandparents for the first time.

I prefer a tighter coil on my fusilli

Even though we ate in shifts, children and parents came together in the kitchen for Saturday dinner, which made the night feel as special as mom's Alfredo. My parents worked late during the week; it was on the weekends that I got Carole's food. I coveted fusilli. I loved the way the spirals stretched and bounced off the end of my fork, and how the sauce found its way into the loops. At the table, I added even more Parm and lots of black pepper, then prepared to defend my portion against the incoming dad attacks. Frank would arm himself with his own fork and circle us, then swoop in like a seagull.

After the last of my fusilli had been stabbed and dragged through any sauce left in the bowl, I was off to watch the epic double-header of *Love Boat* and *Fantasy Island*. Starch, butter, cheese, love, fantasy: Saturday nights were peak living.

As a parent with my own young children, I, too, came home late on weeknights, after Leo and Cosmo had eaten dinner with their babysitter. I knew having a career was important and essential—good!—but not making their dinner felt like a fail. At the time, my working-mom friends all agreed that guilt was one of the defining emotions of motherhood. Meal planning was one way I tried to compensate and stay connected. Even if I wasn't there for dinner, I'd have premade part of it on the weekend, or I'd decided what they should eat, made sure the shopping got done, and printed out recipes for our sitters. It was a conceptual link that I clung to.

I cooked on the weekends—just like my mom did—and the four of us usually ate together, too. At some point on Saturday or Sunday afternoon, I'd extricate myself from kid duties to start cooking. I can hear myself telling little Leo that I couldn't do Legos or play cards because *Mommy's hands are busy right now*. It was the noblest of excuses; after all, we had to eat.

I shopped and cooked for my sons and my husband with consistency, kept them well, nourished them, tried hard to give them comfort and care. Even if I didn't own it then, I retreated to the kitchen (and the supermarket) under the guise of providing and claimed that time for myself. I needed an outlet and a pursuit—we all do—and if I was cooking out of love, it meant I wouldn't have another thing to feel bad about. It was both selfish and giving, and I wonder if it was the same for Carole as she made not one but two dinners on Saturday nights. Cooking was my free pass. Other spouses drop off the laundry, or weed the lawn, or go to the car wash and call friends on the drive.

Before the separation, I didn't recognize that my instinct to cook was a need to create. As annoying as it was to unpack the groceries after shopping, transforming them into something we could eat was my biggest flex. My role in the kitchen gave me a sense of power and pride. I chose it, after all. Preparing food for others helped me connect with the creative satisfaction I get from turning food into meals, and it developed the skills that are how I earn my money. I still have some regrets about time, but I no longer carry guilt about what I was doing in the kitchen, alone.

My kids know Alfredo as "cheesy pasta," but it's the same thing. I favor De Cecco fusilli, the same brand Carole had in the pantry—the coils just feel right. My galley kitchen is open on one end, so anyone can watch me make it, but my back is turned when I'm at the range. Will my children remember what the back of my body looks like, the way I remember my mom's? Maybe so. It is what it is. I have to watch what's happening while I do the stirring and the splashing and the cheese-adding. If the butter starts to look greasy, that means the emulsion isn't holding. Add more pasta water. If the sauce is runny, it needs more cheese. If the cheese starts to look stringy, there's too much heat in the pot; pull it onto the counter to cool down. This is focused time.

Within a few minutes of stirring, the fat from the butter and the cheese should become one with the liquid you've added, and the ridges of the pasta will look like they've been dipped in sauce. That's when you should taste it for salt and pepper. Go time. Yes, I had to leave the room to do this, but now I'm back, so get your asses in seats. I've got a big pot of pasta, and I can't wait to hear you tell me that I make it the best.

Saturday Night Alfredo
Serves 4

Kosher salt

8 ounces Parmigiano, plus more for serving

1 pound fusilli

8 tablespoons (4 ounces/ 1 stick) unsalted butter, cut into pieces

Freshly ground pepper

Bring a large pot of salted water to a boil for the pasta.

In the meantime, break the Parm into a few pieces and blend them in a blender or mini chopper on low speed until the cheese is in small beads, about 30 seconds. Set the blender Parm aside. (Alternatively, use a food processor. Or, grate the cheese on the large holes of a box grater, then finely chop. All of these methods are preferable to using a Microplane.)

Add the pasta to the boiling water and cook for a minute or two less than package instructions; it should be very al dente and will finish cooking in the sauce. Scoop out about 2 cups pasta water, then drain the fusilli and return the pasta to the hot pot. Add the butter and stir until it's melted and coats the noodles.

Gradually add the blender Parm, stirring constantly and adding splashes of pasta water as needed to help the cheese melt. The residual heat of the pot should be more than sufficient to melt the cheese; keep stirring and adding cheese. Once all of the cheese has been added, stir until the sauce is creamy and blankets the noodles completely. Pasta water will give the cheese something to emulsify into; use it to adjust the consistency of the sauce.

Taste the pasta and season the Alfredo with a few grinds of pepper and additional salt, if needed. Serve with more cheese for passing at the table.

New Skin

I was melting sugar for crème caramel when I got my first real burn. I was twenty-six years old and a student at the French Culinary Institute in downtown Manhattan.

I'm not sure how or why I was by myself in an empty kitchen classroom that day, but there I was, gently swirling a sugar syrup in the standard-issue saucepan, mesmerized. Caramel is a magical and scientific thing—a mix of water and sugar, placed over heat, that will, with time, change color and flavor as the temperature rises. I watched as though waiting in shallow waters to spear a fish.

As the sugar melted into the water, it formed a viscous and clear syrup, with large bubbles that broke on the surface. It shifted from clear to straw yellow, then hay, then peanut brown, then the color of bourbon, becoming increasingly fluid. When the caramel gave off the first wisp of smoke, the instructions said to pour cream into the pan, which would both stop the cooking process and give the caramel a stretchy, not brittle, texture.

I poured too fast, from too high up. When the cold cream hit the molten sugar, the caramel sputtered, launching an arc of sweet lava that landed on the back of my left hand. For a glorious, dissociated second, my brain didn't register pain. My attempt to wipe the caramel off spread it out more. I shoved my fist under running water, and when I took my hand out, the burned spot was already puffing into a blister. In an instant, my moment alone had flipped into a physical injury that could be measured by degrees.

Without anyone to witness my pain, I did what made sense to me at the time: quit stalling and finish the recipe. I returned the saucepan to the stovetop to melt the hot sugar into the cream and smooth out the sauce. I tilted the sauce into individual ramekins, coating each with a thin layer, my blister on fire. I'm sure the vanilla custard base followed, and then the water bath, the jiggle test, the chilling, and finally, the unmolding. But I only remember standing next to the sink, hot caramel fused to my skin, temporarily lulled while synapses fired. And then, pain that sticks.

An inch away is my second real burn: a jagged line along my thumb joint. I got it at Union Pacific restaurant when my left hand nudged the handle of a cast-iron skillet that had been preheating in a 550°F oven.

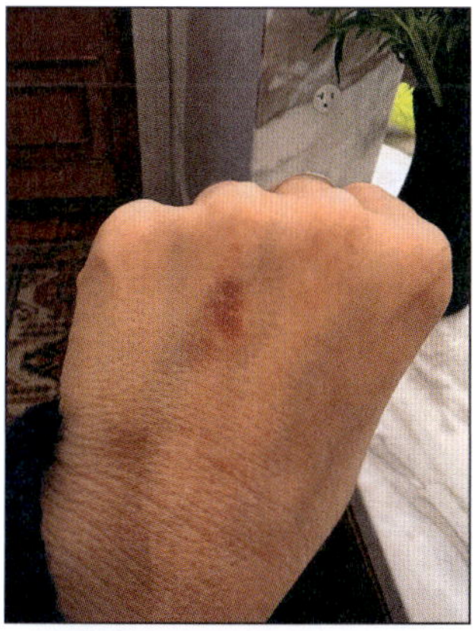

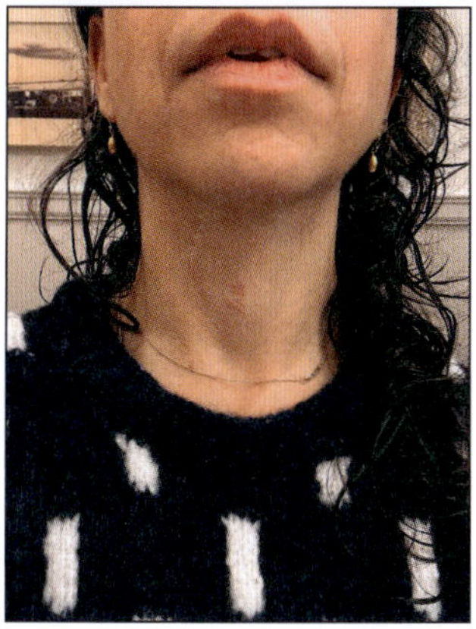

Little burns

That time, the top layer of my skin fused to the skillet and stayed there when I pulled my hand away. Another split second of wonderment before my brain caught up with my eyes, but I was in the middle of service. There were cooks surrounding me, none with sympathy to spare. I spent the rest of the night trying to ignore the sting of salt and lemon juice seasoning my open wound.

At that job, I regularly anointed my forearms with bitty burns that would spring to life when I stepped into the shower at home. I swear my fingerprints have been compromised from stupidly letting my fingers graze fry oil while lowering battered vegetables and doughs into their cauldron. Every knuckle has been blistered by oven racks. I've burned spots on my neck and collarbones from rendering chicken thighs, whose fat exploded upward, schmaltz freckles for life.

My caramel scar is still visible, a reminder that molten sugar is indeed as dangerous as recipes say. That scar also reminds me of the physical changes cooking—this career, life, time—has wrought on my body. It's the theatrical prop I wave around when telling kitchen stories at dinner parties, and yet it amazes me that it's visible when my body has continued to change all around it. I've accumulated more nicks and dents since caramel day, and the pinky on that hand is wonky from a bad break. Sometimes I look down and see my mother's hands.

I can't say this bothers me: being dainty and soft was never my goal. I learned to register and acknowledge pain without overreacting from my burns, and I traded aversion for awe at the body's ability to heal, even when broken blisters look really gnarly. Kitchen injuries granted me admission to the world of gross-out one-upmanship that happens when cooks trade the tales behind their scars. If you think you had it bad, someone else had it worse. My chef at Montrachet had a story about a guy who *died* after a mishap involving fry oil.

The simplest definition of cooking is heat plus time. My cooking scars are high heat for the briefest moment, yet they've stayed with me through decades. The job I chose came with a promise of injury, in ways big and small. Hypothetically, the more injuries I amassed, the more experience I'd gained. If your workplace is covered in knives and surrounded by fire, you're going to get hurt. In the twisted logic of line cook brain, a burn is another entry on the resume. Sometimes I look at my scars and feel proud of that tough young cook; other times I wonder, what was she thinking?

My scars inspire nostalgia for younger Carla, who was midstride in seminal experiences, though at the time I was just trying to get through one more shift. Then, every burn shocked. Each one stuck. These discolored marks take me back to each place, each fragmented memory, where I was, and what I was cooking. I love them for that. They're a smidge of danger, a dash of thoughtlessness, a momentary lapse, an open oven door, a shimmering pot of oil, pools of fat in a skillet, and bragging rights for life.

Culinary School Crème Caramel
Makes eight 4-ounce servings

Adapted from the French Culinary Institute

For the Caramel

1 cup (192g) sugar

1 teaspoon fresh lemon juice

Flaky salt, for seasoning

For the Custard Base

2 cups (500ml) whole milk

Pinch of kosher salt

½ vanilla bean, split lengthwise

3 large eggs

¾ cup (144g) sugar

Preheat the oven to 325°F. Line a glass baking dish or roasting pan with parchment paper. Place eight 6-ounce ramekins in the dish or pan.

Make the caramel:
In a small, deep heavy-bottomed saucepan, combine the sugar, lemon juice, and 2 tablespoons water. Stir until no dry spots remain; mixture will resemble heavy, wet sand. Place over low heat and cook, stirring, until the sugar is mostly dissolved but the liquid is still slightly cloudy, 5 minutes. (Giving the sugar time to dissolve before the liquid simmers will prevent crystallization, a technical mishap that halts the development of the caramel.)

Cover the pot and cook, checking frequently, until the liquid is clear and small, active bubbles are breaking evenly over the surface, about 5 minutes more.

Uncover the pot and nudge up the heat to medium. Cook, swirling the liquid occasionally, until the syrup is the color of hay, 4 to 5 minutes. Continue to cook, gently swirling the liquid occasionally, until the caramel progresses from the color of peanut skins to toasted walnut, 3 to 5 minutes, at which point you should also see wisps of smoke.

Immediately and carefully pour the caramel into the ramekins, dividing evenly. Pick up each ramekin and tilt it to coat the surface and come a bit of the way up the sides with caramel. Return the ramekins to the baking dish and season each with a pinch of flaky salt. Let sit while you make the custard.

Make the custard base:
Bring a kettle of water to a boil for the water bath.

In a medium saucepan, combine milk and kosher salt. Scrape in the vanilla seeds and add the ½ pod. Set over medium heat.

While the milk is warming, in a medium bowl, gently whisk together the eggs and sugar until the mixture is homogeneous and glassy-looking, about 3 minutes. Avoid aerating the mixture: Make sure the whisk stays in contact with the bottom of the bowl while it's moving around, rather than beating with it up and over the surface. This reduces air bubbles in the baked custards and makes them ultra-silky.

When the milk is steaming hot with small bubbles around the edge of the pan, gradually ladle it into the egg mixture, whisking constantly until all of the milk has been added, then pour it through a fine-mesh sieve into a large spouted measuring cup. Pour the custard into the caramel-lined ramekins, coming just below the lip (you may have a little custard left over).

Open the oven and set the baking sheet on the middle rack. Pour hot water into the baking dish to come halfway up the sides of the ramekins.

Bake until the crème caramels are mostly set but jiggle a bit at the very center when jostled, and a paring knife comes out clean, 30 to 35 minutes.

Let them cool in the water bath for 30 minutes, then remove. Cover ramekins with a sheet of plastic wrap and refrigerate until completely cooled, at least 4 hours and up to 2 days.

To unmold, run a thin-bladed knife around the edge of the custard, making sure the tip of the knife reaches all the way down to the caramel layer. Invert a small plate over a ramekin, then quickly turn the plate and ramekin over, holding them together securely as you invert so that things don't slip around. Place the plate on a surface and slowly lift up the ramekin. The custard should slide out, with caramel cascading over the top. If not, place the ramekin back onto the plate and hold them firmly together while you give the plate a few swift downward shakes until the crème caramel releases.

*Things I Cooked for Myself When I Didn't Feel Like Shopping**

*or cooking, to be honest

Canned chickpeas with lemon on lemon (page 172). Ham and cheese, on a bagel, with spicy mayo and mustard. Turkey and cheese, on a bagel, with spicy mayo and pickles. Banana and crunchy peanut butter, with flaky salt (standing up). Mortadella roll-ups with string cheese (standing up). Farro with kimchi and good stock, with fried bread. Ramen noodles with kimchi and tofu (page 164). Bucatini with little pieces of leftover duck confit from Christmas. Oatmeal with apricots, brown sugar, salted peanuts, and butter. Salad sandwich with sharp cheddar (page 168). Tuna salad (a lot), on Triscuits or on toast. Celery salad with black vinegar, fish sauce, and chili crisp. Soba with instant dashi, a jammy egg, and chili crisp. Melted broccoli pasta. Broccoli D. (IYKYK), on rice. Red cabbage salad with grated garlic, red wine vinegar, olive oil, and Parm. Popcorn for dinner (page 206) with *Below Deck* or *Vanderpump Rules*. Crisped-up sweet potato with yogurt and chili crisp (page 231). Aglio e olio with fridge-foraged greens (page 179). Braised firm tofu from H Mart (standing up). Banana bread with cocoa and peanuts (page 169).

H MART
39 3RD AVE
NY, NY 10003
646-596-7755
PAYMENT METHOD : *VISA
DATE TIME : 5/3/2025
RECEIPT #
CASHIER : MANISHA
REGISTER # : REG01
PRIMA SINGAPORE LAKSA 26.4OZ F $ 17.99
** 013934067988
HEALTH ADE KOMBUCHA PASSION FRUIT 16OZ TF $ 5.49
** 851861006867 $ 0.05
** BOTTLE DEPOIST
BBQ GOLDEN ORIGINAL BONELESS T $ 14.99
** 0207
GREAT LAKES MINI CUCUMBER 1LB F $ 3.49
** 673992100081
** Reg Prc: $$3.49 / Savings: $$0.00
JINGA STEWED TOFU 16OZ F $ 7.99
** 6131
ORGANIC HASS AVOCADOS
** 94225
H MART
39 3RD AVE
NY, NY 10003
646-596-7755
PAYMENT METHOD : *VISA
DATE TIME : 4/26/2025 1:50:10 PM
RECEIPT # : 279727701
CASHIER : MANISHA
REGISTER # : REG01
OREO CHOCOLATE CREAM 100G
** 8801037088205 F $ 4.49
BS SESAME OIL 320ML
** 8801007441375 F $ 14.49
SOYBEAN SPROUTS, USA 12OZ
** 028346071409 F $ 2.99
** Reg Prc: $$2.99 / Savings: $$0.00
H MART KIMCHI ONIGIRI
** 0915 TF $ 3.49
H MART TUNA KIMBAB
** 0514 TF $ 8.99
ANGUS BEEF FINGER MEAT
** 1196 F $ 8.83
H MART PRIME BEEF SKIRT MEAT
** 1435 F $ 9.45
ORGANIC HASS AVOCADOS
** 94225 F $ 7.00
** 2 @ 3.99
** Reg Prc: $$7.98 / Savings: $$0.98
NUTTY SESAME CRUNCH 7OZ
** 804846001814 TF $ 5.49
PMO ORGANIC TWO CUP TOFU FIRM 15.5OZ
** 753214109068 F $ 3.49
** Reg Prc: $$3.49 / Savings: $$0.00
T = STATE TAX ITEM
F = FOODSTAMP ITEM
SUB TOTAL $ 68.71
SALES TAX $ 1.59
TOTAL $ 70.30
SALE
DateTime : 4/26/2025 13:54:17
Card Type : VISA
Account : 5212
Entry Mode : Contactless
ReceiptTotal : $70.30
Batch # : 2
Auth Code : 095013
Transaction # : 144
Response : AUTH/TKT
HostCode : N/A
APPLAB : VISA DEBIT
H MART
39 3RD AVE
NY, NY 10003
646-596-7755
2:06:37 PM
AJAY
REG02
F $ 3.49
F $ 5.99
TF $ 5.49
$ 0.05
F $ 3.49
F $ 4.49
F $ 2.49
F $ 2.49
3.49
F $ 9.99
F $ 13.99
TF $ 8.49
F $ 8.49
TF $ 3.99
TF $ 3.49
F $ 10.99
F $ 2.99
BAY LEAVES F $ 5.49
** 3204
AMERICAN CHIVE F $ 3.99
HOLLAND RED LONG F $ 4.99
SHANGHAI TIP F $ 4.41
** 3147
H MART GARLIC F $ 4.03
** 4608
F $ 3.23
SUB TOTAL $ 120.03
SALES TAX $ 1.90
TOTAL $ 121.93
H MART
39 3RD AVE
NY, NY 10003
5/20/2025 10:57:02 AM
H MART CRAB MEAT KIMBAB
** 0501
H MART MENTAIKO ONIGIRI
** 0904
FERRERO ROCHER
COFFEE(L)
** 10023204
T = STATE TAX ITEM
F = FOODSTAMP ITEM
MART
39 3RD AVE
NY, NY 10003
646-596-7755
/5/2025 2:23:32 PM
RICE 2LB
F $ 4.99
F $ 4.99
F $ 2.49
F $ 2.49
F $ 2.49
F $ 2.49
F $ 9.37
PAYMENT METHOD : *VISA
DATE TIME
RECEIPT #
CASHIER
REGISTER #
1:52:11 PM
T $ 2.49
F $ 7.99
F $ 5.99
F $ 5.99
F $ 5.49
F $ 6.49

Tofu and Kimchi Soup with Noodles
For 1, with leftovers

Any type of cooking oil or rendered fat

½ onion, chopped

Kosher salt

Heaping cup of cabbage kimchi

Spoonful of gochujang

1 serving bouillon paste or cube

½ package firm tofu, cut into spoon-friendly shapes

3 ounces dried ramen or other wheat noodle

Fish sauce and soy sauce, for seasoning

Toasted sesame oil, for drizzling

Heat a big spoonful of oil or fat in a medium saucepot over medium-high. Add the onion, season with salt, and cook, stirring, until soft, a few minutes. Add the kimchi and its liquid and fry in the oil until the kimchi liquid has reduced and the cabbage pieces are hot and sizzling. A little browning at the edges is nice, too.

Add the gochujang—more than a tablespoon if you want this pretty spicy, less if not. Cook, stirring, to caramelize the gochujang a bit. Add about 3 cups water and the bouillon, or use stock, or just plain water. Simmer gently until the liquid starts to taste like something, maybe 10 to 15 minutes.

Add the tofu and continue to simmer gently to develop flavors, 8 to 10 minutes.

Meanwhile, cook the noodles. Transfer them to a deep soup bowl. Taste the soup and adjust seasoning with fish sauce and soy sauce. Ladle the soup over the noodles and drizzle with sesame oil.

Salad Sandwich
Makes 2 sandwiches

3 tablespoons extra-virgin olive oil

3 tablespoons fresh lemon juice

1 tablespoon Dijon mustard

2 teaspoons honey

Kosher salt; freshly ground pepper

Distilled white vinegar, for seasoning

Big handful of sturdy lettuce leaves, such as red leaf or iceberg, torn in half if large

Softened unsalted butter, for the bread

4 slices thin-crusted sandwich bread or 2 rolls, lightly toasted if desired

10 thin slices sharp cheddar cheese, from a block, or 6 deli-style slices

In a small jar, combine the oil, lemon juice, mustard, and honey. Season generously with salt and pepper, then close up the jar and shake the dressing until emulsified. Taste and adjust the seasoning with vinegar and more salt and pepper, if needed.

Toss the lettuce leaves in a medium bowl with enough dressing to coat generously (you'll have enough dressing for 4 sandwiches). Season with salt. Butter top side of each slice of bread from wall to wall, then shingle cheese on two of the slices, dividing evenly. Top the other slices with salad, then close the sandwiches up.

Banana Bread with Cocoa and Salted Peanuts

Makes 1 loaf

Softened butter, for the pan

1¾ cups (210g) all-purpose flour

2 tablespoons (14g) unsweetened cocoa powder

2 teaspoons (6g) kosher salt

1½ teaspoons (9g) baking soda

1 cup (192g) dark brown sugar, not packed

½ cup (96g) granulated sugar

12 tablespoons (170g/ 1½ sticks) butter

4 large very ripe bananas (1½ pounds total)

2 large eggs

¼ cup salted roasted peanuts, roughly chopped

2 tablespoons turbinado sugar

Flaky salt

Preheat the oven to 375°F. Butter a 10 × 5-inch loaf pan, preferably metal, then line it with parchment (if your pan measures 9 × 5-inch, use that; bake time may be ever-so-slightly longer). Let the parchment overhang on the long sides, trimming excess.

In a medium bowl, toss together the flour, cocoa, salt, and baking soda. In a large bowl, combine the brown sugar and granulated sugar. Melt the butter just until foaming, then pour the butter over the sugars. Stir to combine.

Mash the bananas in a medium bowl until shiny and loose, then whisk in the eggs. Wait until the butter mixture has cooled a bit, then add the banana mixture and whisk to combine. Add the flour mixture and fold together just until no floury bits remain.

Scrape the batter into the pan and smooth the top. Sprinkle the peanuts over, then the turbinado sugar, then some flaky salt. Place the loaf pan on a rimmed baking sheet and transfer to the oven.

Bake until the top is very dark brown, firm, and almost burned at the corners, 1 hour 25 minutes to 1 hour 35 minutes. (If you're using a glass baking dish, turn on convection for the first half hour, if that's an option.) A cake tester should come out clean; if you have a digital thermometer, check at dead center—it's fully cooked at 210°F. If the bread is underbaked, it will buckle and the center will be claggy.

Let the banana bread cool in the pan for 30 minutes. Lift it out of the pan, peel off the parchment, and leave it be on a rack until completely cooled. Lovingly and patiently place your hands on the long sides to check for warmth. This is even better the next day. I like it well-toasted, slathered with softened butter or cream cheese, and a little salt.

Lemony Chickpea Stew with Rice
4 servings

For the Stew

2 lemons

⅓ cup extra-virgin olive oil

6 garlic cloves, thinly sliced

4 celery stalks, cut into small dice

2 medium leeks, sliced into ½-inch-thick rounds, rinsed and blotted dry

Kosher salt; freshly ground pepper

2 (15.5-ounce) cans chickpeas, drained and rinsed

1 teaspoon coriander seeds, crushed

1 teaspoon dried dill

1 teaspoon dried mint

¾ teaspoon crushed red pepper flakes

½ cup long-grain white rice, rinsed

4 cups chicken or vegetable stock

For the Magic Green Sauce and Serving

Ice

4 big handfuls of mature spinach, trimmed and roughly chopped

2 cups mixed loosely packed herbs, such as cilantro, dill, and/or chives

½ cup nutritional yeast

¼ cup extra-virgin olive oil

1 garlic clove

Kosher salt; freshly ground pepper

For Serving

Greek yogurt

1 lemon, cut into wedges

Olive oil, for drizzling

Crushed red pepper flakes

Kosher salt; freshly ground pepper

Make the stew:
Use a vegetable peeler to remove the zest in wide strips from 1 lemon. Squeeze ¼ cup of juice from that lemon, and possibly 1 more. Set zest and juice aside, separately.

Heat a heavy deep skillet with a lid or 4-quart Dutch oven over medium. Add the olive oil, garlic, celery, and leeks. Season with salt and pepper and cook, stirring frequently, until the vegetables get juicy, about 3 minutes. Cover the pot and cook until the leeks soften, 3 to 5 minutes. Uncover, allowing steam to drip back into the pot, and increase the heat to medium-high. Cook, stirring, until the garlic is light golden.

Lower the heat to medium, add the chickpeas, and stir to coat. Add the coriander, dill, mint, pepper flakes, and strips of zest. Stir to bloom the spices. Stir in the rice. Add the stock and 2 tablespoons lemon juice (save the rest of the juice for the sauce). Bring the liquid to a simmer, then cover the pot, lower the heat to medium-low, and cook gently until the rice is tender, about 15 minutes.

Make the Magic Green Sauce:
Place two ice cubes into a blender jar and top with the spinach, herbs, nutritional yeast, olive oil, and the remaining 2 tablespoons lemon juice. Finely grate the garlic right into the mix and season with salt and pepper. Blend until smooth and emulsified, about 2 minutes (the ice helps keep the mixture green). Add water by the tablespoon if needed to get the blades turning. Transfer the sauce to a bowl; you should have about 1 cup or a bit more. Taste and season the sauce as needed.

Check the stew for seasoning; loosen if desired with more stock or hot water.

Serve the stew topped with a big spoonful each of yogurt and Magic Green Sauce, lemon wedges, a drizzle of olive oil, a pinch of pepper flakes, and some salt and pepper.

Parental Praise

When I was in college, I knew how to make exactly two pasta dishes: aglio e olio and cacio e pepe. This and that, and that and this.

Aglio e olio, if you don't know, is simply garlic and oil. Lots of the first, and extra-virgin of the other. Lightly toast garlic slices in the oil, season with salt and pepper, and use that to dress pasta. *Finita*. Even my dad, Frank, who used paring knives to sharpen his editing pencils, had the panache to whip this one together—a testament to its simplicity.

Cacio e pepe is cheese and pepper, copious amounts of both, that you stir into barely drained pasta after coating it in olive oil. As you stir and add pasta water, the cheese melts and becomes a sauce that fuses to the noodles. Pecorino cheese is typical; at the regular-ass grocery store in Providence, Rhode Island, where I was a flannel-wearing, Foucault-reading undergrad at Brown, they stocked Locatelli Romano. So I bought that. Years later, food editors I worked with at *Bon Appétit* would dismiss it as too salty, too funky, too crude. College Carla thought it was great.

The interventions I brought to both dishes were what my mom always did at home: add a vegetable. For aglio e olio, I leaned on the mustard family: curly kale, mature arugula, broccoli, and broccoli rabe. Sometimes Swiss chard. Rarely spinach. I'd soften the greens in the oil and garlic and dress the finished dish with Parm. Mac and cheese, but make it healthy. Easy enough.

For cacio e pepe, I landed on green beans and never left. I cut them into 1-inch lengths and threw them in with the pasta toward the end of the cooking so that they'd be tender at the same time. I'd dump the pasta and green beans into a colander together, slide them back in the pot, and mix my cheesy sauce in the residual heat. I liked twisty noodles that would lasso the clusters of cheese—fusilli, radiatore, casarecce.

Eventually, I Frankensteined the two techniques. I'd cook garlic in oil à la aglio e olio and use that to dress my pasta and beans before adding the pecorino. It wasn't a big intervention as far as recipes go—all I was doing was infusing the oil with garlic—but it amounted to a twist on a classic

(or two). The purpose of cooking then was to get full, and I liked how this tasted. I ate it a lot without giving much credit to my creativity.

Around that time, I remember telling Frank about the hybrid recipe I was making in my off-campus apartment. He was a magazine editor who specialized in personal finance. I had no idea what a mutual fund was, and he couldn't give a shit about Jacques Derrida. I knew that talking to him about food was going to be a lot more interesting than trying to explain my deconstructive feminist reading of *Pride and Prejudice*. Despite the divide, I actively sought his approval (still do). I was raised in a "we're not mad, we're just disappointed" household, where a so-so report card could *reallllly* bring the mood down. Over time, I exceeded expectations, performing my achievements for attention and affection. (I've not *not* talked about this in therapy.)

Carole and Frank at their dining table

Food was a new way in. We loved food! Still do. Getting better as a cook was my way of showing him I had become self-reliant, was eating my veggies, and was carrying on the maternal cooking gene. What magazine editor wouldn't love that storyline? But what came out of his mouth next surprised me. In his reporter's way, he said, *Let me get this straight: You're taking the garlic and oil from one dish and putting it with the cheese and pepper from the other, and adding green beans?*

Yeah, and it's really good.

Switching to his fatherly get-ready-to-receive-praise way, he looked me in the eyes and said, *You invented a new dish.* Outwardly, I scoffed and downplayed my accomplishment (who was I??). Inwardly, I glowed. This was the first time he'd acknowledged my cooking skills, and already he'd given me author credit on my first original recipe. I felt a glimmer of artistic pride in my survival-mode pasta. No clue what I put in that Jane Austen essay, though.

I still feel a little puffed up when I make cacio e pepe e green beans. I spoon up some of that coveted Frankie applause every time. What could have been small talk, one conversation of many that we had about what I was doing at school, managed to foreshadow the work I'd grow into as a food writer decades later. I've developed dozens of pasta recipes since then—slow-cooked ragus, hand-shaped noodles with butter and lemon, and lavish sauces with crispy mushrooms—but I never forgot about this one. It's remained a staple in my home cooking, the recipe and its method evolving with me over time, and it's now way better than I remember.

Aglio, Olio e Everything
3 or 4 servings

1 bunch of kale (any type), broccoli, broccoli rabe, mustard greens, Swiss chard, mature arugula, or mature spinach, trimmed and roughly chopped

⅓ cup extra-virgin olive oil

10 garlic cloves, sliced not-too-thin

2 anchovy fillets (optional)

1 teaspoon crushed red pepper flakes, plus more for serving

Kosher salt; freshly ground pepper

1 pound spaghetti

Parmigiano, for serving

Bring a large pot of salted water to a boil. Cook the greens until just tender, 4 to 6 minutes depending on which vegetable you're using. Reserve the water for cooking pasta. (If using arugula or spinach, skip this step—it's tender as is and doesn't benefit from being blanched.)

Meanwhile, in a Dutch oven or large skillet, combine the oil and garlic over medium heat and cook, stirring occasionally, until bubbles appear and the garlic is starting to turn translucent, 2 to 3 minutes. Add the anchovies (if using) and pepper flakes and stir until the anchovies disintegrate, about 1 minute. Season with salt and pepper (I like a lot of pepper).

Use a spider to transfer the greens to the garlic mixture and cook, stirring and tossing to coat greens with oil, until the garlic is light golden brown and softened, 3 to 4 minutes more.

Cook the pasta for 2 to 3 minutes less than the package instructions (it should be very al dente and will finish cooking in the sauce).

Scoop out about 1½ cups of pasta cooking liquid, then drain the spaghetti and transfer to the Dutch oven, along with ½ cup of the pasta water. Bring to a simmer over medium heat and cook, tossing constantly with tongs and adding more pasta water as needed, until the pasta is al dente and the sauce is just thick enough to coat the pasta, but there's still plenty of extra sauce in skillet, 2 to 3 minutes. Taste and adjust seasoning with salt as needed.

Serve with more red pepper flakes and Parmigiano for grating over.

College Carla's Pasta with Pecorino and Green Beans

2 servings

8 ounces short pasta, such as casarecce or strozzapreti

6 ounces green beans or haricots verts, trimmed, cut into 2-inch pieces

¼ cup extra-virgin olive oil, plus more for drizzling

4 garlic cloves, thinly sliced

1 cup freshly grated Pecorino Romano, Parmigiano, or a mix (about 1½ ounces), plus more for serving

1 teaspoon freshly ground pepper, plus more for serving

Bring a large pot of salted water to a boil—go a little lighter than usual, since the cheese is salty. Add the pasta and cook until it's a couple of minutes away from al dente. Add the green beans and continue cooking until the pasta is al dente and the beans are bright green and just tender, 1 to 2 minutes. Reserving 1 cup of pasta water, drain the pasta and beans in a colander. Reserve the pot you used for cooking. Don't shake all the water off the pasta; some residual liquid will help form the sauce.

While the pasta is cooking, in a small saucepan, combine the oil and garlic and place over medium heat. Cook, stirring occasionally, until the garlic slices are soft and just beginning to turn golden brown, 4 or 5 minutes. Shoot for the paler side of golden.

Return the pasta and beans to the pot and scrape the garlic mixture over. Stir and toss to coat with oil. Let sit for a minute or two to cool slightly (this will prevent the cheese from clumping), then gradually stir in the pecorino and 1 teaspoon pepper until the pasta is evenly coated with cheese. If the pasta looks dry and/or greasy, correct with splashes of pasta water. If the cheese begins to clump and stick to the spoon, let it cool a minute or two, then go again.

Serve pasta topped with another drizzle of oil, some pepper, and additional grated pecorino.

BARTHES IMAGE MUSIC TEXT

In Defense of Not-Flaky Biscuits

I had been working at food magazines for a few years when I found out that tall, flaky, layered biscuits were "a thing."

I'd eaten my share of biscuits, but I hadn't yet been schooled on the biscuit hierarchy: round and fluffy versus square and stacked. Did *you* know that the biscuit you prefer determines what kind of person you are??

(As an aside: No group of people was more dedicated to semantic food shaming than the staff at *Bon Appétit* when I worked there in the 2010s. Forget biscuits. We had *screaming* fights about artichokes. What is the most upsetting pasta shape and why is it angel hair?)

Now that polyamory has become mainstream, I would like to declare my ability to love many types of biscuits equally and at the same time. I grew up on my mother's diminutive, circular, tender golden-brown biscuits that she still bakes in the same 10-inch cast-iron skillet. You can pull the top and bottom apart, but they don't split into pastry-like layers—the crumb is homogeneous and usually flecked with cornmeal. She throws them together on weekend mornings before anyone else has woken up; nothing beats rolling into a kitchen and spotting a skillet full of biscuits sitting on the stovetop. That's love.

A batch of Carole's cornmeal biscuits

Over the years, I've tweaked Carole's recipe, which she adapted from Marion Cunningham. I started adding hard-boiled egg yolks to the dough when I read about that in a Claudia Fleming recipe. Along with the butter, the fat-rich yolks encase the flour, slowing the absorption of water, which reduces gluten. Less gluten, less chew. More delicate.

At some point I got it in my head to make a blackberry cobbler topped with blackberry jam-filled biscuit dough. So I worked on that, and the recipe follows. The dough is rolled out, divided in half, and put back together with a thick layer of jam in between. Cutting the dough into strips encourages it to twist while it bakes, and it comes out looking like it's been topped with whimsical striped ribbons. Babka-esque.

The biscuit I chose for this cobbler is pillowy—a couch cushion filled with cotton balls. (For a ham and pickle sandwich, I'd go for sturdy and flaky.) In a dessert, the serving spoon should be met with no resistance as it moves through the topping and sinks into the fruit underneath. Regarding the dairy product that's leaning against the self-saucing berries on your plate: Whipped cream, crème fraîche, sour cream, vanilla ice cream, a drizzle of cold cream? Yes, yes, yes, yes, yes.

Black-and-Blue Cobbler with Jam Biscuits
8 servings

For the Biscuits

2¼ cups (270g) all-purpose flour

1 tablespoon (12g) sugar

1 teaspoon (3g) kosher salt

2 teaspoons baking powder

½ teaspoon baking soda

2 hard-boiled egg yolks, from large eggs

12 tablespoons (6 ounces/170g/1½ sticks) cold unsalted butter, cut into ½-tablespoon pieces

¾ cup (175ml) cold buttermilk, plus more for brushing

½ cup (160g) blackberry jam

For the Filling

1½ pounds (680g) blueberries (about 4 cups)

1½ pounds (680g) blackberries (about 4 cups)

¾ cup (144g) plus 2 tablespoons (24g) sugar, divided

2 tablespoons cornstarch

1 teaspoon kosher salt

Zest and juice of 1 lime

Buttermilk, for brushing

Whipped cream, cold heavy cream, crème fraîche, sour cream, and/or vanilla ice cream, for serving

Preheat the oven to 350°F. Line a rimmed baking sheet with foil or parchment paper.

Make the biscuits:
In a food processor, combine the flour, sugar, salt, baking powder, baking soda, and egg yolks and pulse until the yolks are in small pieces, about 12 pulses. Add the butter and pulse until the butter is in very small beads and the mixture resembles cornmeal, 35 to 40 pulses. For a flaky biscuit (or pie dough, for that matter), you'd leave the butter in larger pieces so that they create pockets of steam and layered texture in the final biscuit. For these, you want the butter and flour to create a sandy texture, which yields a tender, more homogeneous crumb. Stream in the buttermilk while pulsing and pulse just enough to bring the dough together.

Turn out the dough onto a lightly floured work surface (or parchment paper). With a lightly floured rolling pin, roll out the dough to a roughly 9 × 12-inch rectangle, ¼ inch thick. With a long side facing you, cut dough in half crosswise. Spread the jam evenly onto one piece of dough, then place the other piece of dough on top, like a sandwich.

Cut the jam-filled dough in half lengthwise to make 2 strips about 9 × 3 inches. Then cut each of those long pieces crosswise to create ¾-inch-wide strips. (If at any point the dough warms up or becomes difficult to handle, chill for 10 minutes to firm up.) Transfer the strips to the lined baking sheet and chill while you make the filling.

> **Get ahead:** The dough can be rolled out, filled with jam, and cut into strips up to 3 days ahead. Wrap airtight and refrigerate. (Alternatively, freeze for up to 2 months.)

Make the filling:
In a large bowl, combine both berries, ¾ cup sugar, cornstarch, and salt. Finely grate the lime zest over, then halve the lime and squeeze in the juice. Gently toss until no dry spots remain, then use a large fork to lightly crush about a third of the berries. Taste the mixture and adjust sugar and salt as needed. Scrape the mixture into an oval, square, or rectangular 2-quart baking dish, 2 to 3 inches deep, and place on the prepared baking sheet.

Arrange the chilled strips on top of the fruit, twisting them slightly so that the jammy edge is exposed in some spots. Lightly brush the dough with buttermilk and sprinkle the remaining 2 tablespoons sugar over.

Bake until the topping is dark golden brown and fruit juices are bubbling at the surface of the cobbler, about 1 hour 10 minutes. (Loosely cover with aluminum foil if the biscuit topping is sufficiently browned before the juices are bubbling.)

Let the cobbler cool until the side of the baking dish is just warm to the touch. If you spoon into it when it's still hot, the fruit juices will be thin and runny, which is a disservice to them, and to the work you did. This is why we bake in the early part of the day and have cobbler after dinner. (Leftover cobbler is also amazing for breakfast the next day. Loosely cover and leave it at room temperature.)

Serve spoonfuls of cobbler with some whipped cream, a drizzle of cold cream, a dollop of crème fraîche or sour cream, and/or a scoop of vanilla ice cream.

Segments

Growing up, I spent a lot of time at a friend's home at the tip of Long Island, a creaky farmhouse with a rope swing off the side porch and lilac bushes in the back.

Over time, I visited less and less, but I'm often flooded with memories of summers in that borrowed backyard. There's the time I was sitting in the grass with my second child, Cosmo, who was coming up on one, though still a baby to me. Lots of people were there that weekend for a party. Long tables set for dinner filled the backyard, and there were lanterns hanging in the trees.

I was wearing a sarong over my bathing suit, Cosmo in my lap with his back against my belly, kangaroo-style. We were hanging with friends, and the grown-ups were talking. As I chatted away, I fed Cosmo an orange—arms encircling his belly, my busy hands in front of his chest. Without a cutting board, knife, or kitchen, I used what I had—fingers and teeth—to prepare the orange for him. I peeled it under his nose, then started pulling away individual segments. As each segment was liberated from the whole, I'd lift it over Cosmo's head and bite through the thick seam of the membrane at the top, where the segment attaches to the fuzzy core, spitting seeds on the lawn as I went along.

Next, I used my fingertips to peel the membrane from either side of the segment, exposing the compact stack of juice-filled sacs inside. The naked citrus pulp was still girded on the underside by webbed peel. I bent the segment back so that it split into a left and right side, then brought it up to Cosmo's mouth. He'd chomp into the fruit, first one half, then the other. Whatever was left in my hand, I ate—tacky orange-scented pith, the bitter bits and stringy dregs. Having had plenty of oranges in my life, I didn't mind getting stuck with the throwaway parts.

We went through the whole orange like this. I ripped off a segment. Broke the top seam and teased away the sides, held it up to his fat lips. He tipped his chin like a baby deer nibbling grass, and tore off the good part. The juicy vesicles (that's what they're called) burst in his mouth. Over and over. He loved it. I had to speed up to match his enthusiasm for the next

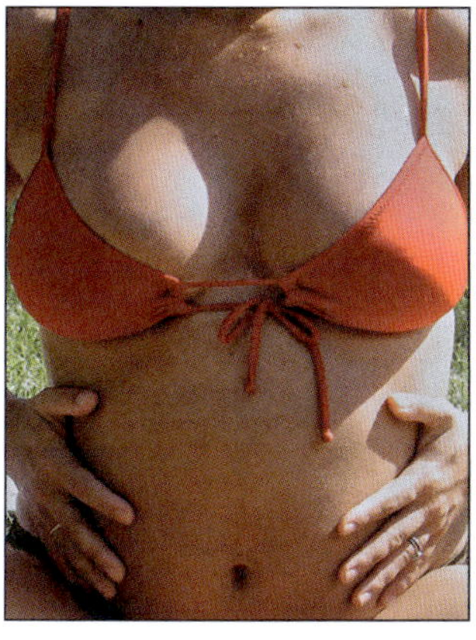

During my first pregnancy

piece. I wished another orange would appear when this one was done, my only chance at keeping this citrus monster in my clutches.

I knew that the second this four-star fruit delivery program concluded, Cosmo would push his hands into my thighs to come to standing, then march off without a look goodbye. This was always his style—fully committed to his bottle until the last bubbly bits of milk were sucked through the rubber nipple, then his head would turn, body followed, and he'd be on his way. He was content to use pincers to collect Cheerios, which I doled out in small piles to keep him at the table longer. When they were gone, so was he.

I bit into the next segment, readied the juicy bits.

At one point, one of my friends—a man—interrupted whatever conversation was happening to say—

Do you see what she's doing?

No one replied.

She's peeling away all of the bad parts and feeding him the fruit, and then she eats the scraps.

His comment made me feel, for a moment, like a species in the wild, telephoto lens trained on a jovial little boho scene. I felt—as they say—seen. I had designed this snack for Cosmo's pleasure, his enrichment, his sustenance. My friend saw my work, but did he see the selfishness in my strategy? I may have been projecting dutiful mother, but my biological and emotional need to keep him close was being met as well.

That day in the grass was only the beginning. I would come to peel grapes for Cosmo, as I had done for his brother, Leo, before him. I stripped peaches of their skins. I plucked the best berries out of the box and slipped them into their perfectly pursed mouths, and I ate the deflated ones stuck to the corners of the cardboard pint container. I bit into apples, then bit the bites into small, skinless pieces, and fed those to them. I removed the cartilage nubs from the ends of chicken drumsticks so they could grasp the bone in their fists and suck on it like a teether. I wanted them to enjoy the berries and the apples and the taste of meat. I wanted the way I love food to embed in them, like teeth marks on chicken bones.

This is how I defined myself as a mother: I'm keeping you alive with my body. Stay with me, sit with me, eat with me. Cosmo's sturdy toddler's back rested on my front; in utero his spine pushed against my protruding belly. The tannic and fragrant citrus oils stuck to my fingers long after he'd scooted off.

As I write this, Cosmo is weeks away from turning fifteen. When this book is published, he'll be seventeen. Last night he used the tines of his fork to methodically tease every strip of tomato skin from his spaghetti sauce and deposit them on the edge of my plate. We laughed about it—*Oh, I'm your discard pile?*—but teasing doesn't move him to get a side bowl. He knows I'm the person who absorbs his rejects: wrinkly fruit skins, bruised apples, worries, complaints, pain. As his fork repeatedly reached across the space between us and another scrap of red skin appeared on the rim of my bowl, I wasn't mad or annoyed. I trained him to do this, after all, and even in my passivity, I have the power to make this meal taste better to him.

After dinner, he hugs me close; he's so tall now that my cheek rests against his chest, big arms encircling my back. He gives me a quick kiss on the top of my head and I smell his manly pine spice deodorant through his shirt. He is my little bird. He's my baby bear. I'll give him the food out of my mouth. I will feed him with my body.

Do you see what she's doing?

With Leo and Cosmo, my sweet loves

Dreaming-of-Summer Citrus Salad
Serves 4

½ medium shallot, thinly sliced crosswise

4-finger pinch of fennel seeds, lightly crushed

Kosher salt; freshly ground black pepper

Distilled white vinegar

3 oranges, such as navel, blood, Cara Cara, and/or Satsuma

4 tangerines and/or clementines

3 celery stalks

12 Castelvetrano olives

Extra-virgin olive oil, for drizzling

Palmful of roasted pistachios or almonds

Aleppo pepper and flaky salt, for seasoning

In a medium bowl, combine the shallot rings and fennel seeds and season with salt and black pepper. Toss and stir until the shallot starts to look wet, then pour in just enough vinegar to coat generously. This is the base of the dressing.

For tight-skinned oranges, like navel and blood oranges, slice off enough from the stem and bottom end to expose the flesh, then upend the fruit and cut away the peel and pith. Slice the denuded oranges crosswise into thin rounds or irregular wedges. If using a Satsuma, peel it by hand, remove any particularly thick, stringy bits or pieces of pith, and then cut it into similar shapes. Play around with your knife work; make it pretty; they don't all have to be the same. Transfer the oranges to the shallot mixture, but don't toss them together. Peel the tangerines and/or clementines, then separate into clusters of 3 or 4 sections, removing any especially egregious stringy bits. Cut the clusters in half on an angle and add to shallot mixture (don't stir).

Thinly slice the celery on a steep diagonal and add to bowl. Smash the olives with the flat side of the blade, remove the pit, and use your fingers to tear into smaller pieces. Set the olives aside.

Drizzle enough olive oil over the ingredients to generously coat them, season with salt and black pepper, and very gently fold together with your hands or a spoon. Taste and adjust seasoning and oil as needed. Arrange the salad on a serving plate or divide it between two smaller plates. A bowl is not the move here. Scatter the olives and pistachios over, season generously with Aleppo pepper and a couple of pinches of flaky salt, and finish it off with one last shiny drizzle of oil.

5. Snacks for Sharing with Yourself

granola
MONTRACHET
239 WEST BROADWAY • NEW YORK • NY 10013
212-219-2777
CHOC. PLANT PROTEIN
going from being student
to being professional
comfort
confidence
drinks

TAX .00 BAL 67.80
SWIPED
APPROVED
AMOUNT: $67.80
PBBBC smoothie
opt

Butter on the Counter

In my mother's kitchen, there were always three things on the counter.

She had nice crusty bread, whether fresh, stale, semi-stale, shadowed with mold, or a combination thereof.

A black-and-white ceramic cookie jar in the shape of a panda, whose head lifted off to constantly disappoint you: empty.

And a white ceramic dish of room-temperature, unsalted butter.

In adulthood I have come to recognize that there are many types of kitchens with corresponding personalities. Kitchens with two refrigerators, kitchens with a built-in water spout behind the range, kitchens with a vinegar mother floating in a jar in the pantry. Importantly, there are kitchens with butter on the counter, and other kitchens with cold butter in the fridge. Our kitchen had both, which is the correct amount.

I grew up on ordinary Land O'Lakes and never would have thought to complain. We had in-the-moment butter and backup butter, allowing for all eventualities. (If we're being honest, there were additional 1-pound packages of butter in the freezer.) To make biscuits or pie dough with cold pats of butter, you would swing open the fridge door. For toast or an English muffin, you'd want to use soft butter that absorbs right into the nooks. Greasing a loaf pan or cookie sheet for baking is another reason to keep the room-temp stuff at hand.

Countertop butter is useful for these types of practical applications, but its core identity is as what I'd call "snacking butter." Will a snack stave off hunger? Yes. Everybody knows that. But, the true calling of the snack is to create a productive diversion away from that exhausting thing you'd rather not be doing (like, say, writing a book). We must always be prepared to snack: Without it, we might never get anything done. A taxed mind is not a problem-solving mind. The smart thing to do is get up and go into the kitchen, where magical force fields converge to rid us of this mental block. While we wait, we snack.

Carole, my mother, introduced me to two of the greatest butter-adjacent day snacks of all time. The first is a cracker—she likes Stoned Wheat Thins—with soft butter and an anchovy fillet, dressed with freshly cracked pepper. This is what her grandfather, Remo Casini, would eat if he was peckish in the afternoon, and it is indeed what *she* eats when she is peckish in the afternoon. This simple composition has all the things: salt, crunch, mild fattiness, creaminess, funk, and heat.

The other epic snack for the ages is a Dutch pretzel dressed with butter. The Lalli family is fond of Martin's Pretzels, sold at the Union Square Greenmarket. They are flawless: near-burned, bittersweet, and malty, generously speckled with white rock salt. They boast a crumbly hard crunch on the outer humps and a snappy-crisp texture on the thin inner twist. A pretzel, while packing a lot of flavor and sending dramatic crumbs everywhere, is an airy, rather austere thing. The pro move is to gently press your pretzel into the butter so it adheres, as would an elegant dab of moisturizer to a fingertip. Sweet and rich, the butter rounds out and mellows the pretzel's saltiness, and it also melds together all the savory notes. It's perfect, unless other people are around. The butter dish is not a bonfire for huddling. It's a personal chamber candlestick, which you'll snuff when you're ready, and not a moment sooner.

This interlude should be enjoyed—you guessed it—alone, upright in the kitchen, elbows on the countertop, butter lid to the side, gaze unfocused in the middle distance, bag of pretzels within reach. While elemental in nature, this is a noisy, dusty, texturally varied ensemble. The snack pairs well with ruminating thoughts, thoughts you can sift through as you crack into a pretzel with your front bunny teeth and work it into rubble between your molars. Pretzel ears are bigger, capable of delivering lots of butter, but they do have a tendency toward hollowness and are responsible for most of the mess that lands on the counter. Whole pretzels are coveted by some, but true aficionados (like me) enjoy combing through the bag to find a salt-bedecked center X that can be wielded like a pickaxe in the butter.

It's not mindless, what we're doing here. It's an intentional pause, a crunchy one. There will always be difficult things to get back to. Chew on it. Mull it over. Take the off ramp, wander, spend a quiet moment alone. There is no knowing how many pretzels will satisfy your needs, but one is not the right number. When you're done, you're done. Fold the crinkly bag over itself and tuck it away in the cupboard. Then slide the butter dish back into its earned spot on the counter. You'll be back into it soon enough.

Dressed Pretzels
For 1 or more

Pennsylvania Dutch pretzels

Room-temperature butter

Martin's Handmade Pretzels are my preferred pretzel; order them online if you're serious, or go with another Dutch or Pennsylvania-style pretzel. This isn't the time for a pretzel stick or a tiny twist. I'd make an allowance for a sturdy pretzel rod. Love a pretzel rod.

Dip or drag the pretzel, or pretzel fragment, into the softened butter. Consume. There's beauty in the balance between dry and crunchy and soft and luscious, and between crispy-salty and sweet-lactic. You may need to move through a few pretzels before finding the proportion that makes you happiest. Give that to yourself.

I'm Finding It Difficult to Get Any Work Done

I get a kick out of reading the work routines of disciplined, successful writers. You know, the ones who rise at 4 a.m. and write for three hours before their kids get up for school.

Or the Victorian-era ones who "take to their writing chamber" after breakfast and stay in there 'til lunch, then spend the rest of the day on handwritten correspondence. The novelists who go to their desk in the attic and bang it out on typewriters from dawn to dusk, whisky tumbler at the ready.

This is my third book. I have been waiting for some sort of evolution to impact my writing habits—if not "best" practices, a few good ones would be huge. But, no. My process, if you can call it that, is an all-day braise, the slowest rise, the cookie dough that should sit in the fridge for 48 hours before you scoop it. As with any recipe with a lot of inactive time, my work starts with a flurry of action: gathering of beverages, securing of chargers, a playlist selection, brushing of teeth. I'm a very fast touch typist, just look at the speed at which I click through all of my open tabs.

I often need a different beverage from the one I'm drinking, which is how I find myself in the kitchen starting a batch of masala chai. I will think of a good lede while I'm grating ginger.

Writing when hungry will inspire countless delicious ideas. The impulse to make granola, for example. The process is hands-off, like me and my manuscript. If the writing isn't flowing, at least I can make it pour—it being a Neapolitan ice cream–inspired mix of oats, chewy dried sour cherries, nubby pistachios, and slivers of cacao. While the granola bakes, I might as well sit down on the kitchen floor and reorg my pantry. I'm two hours into my writing session—time flies when you're being this productive! I'll be back at the keyboard just as soon as I vacuum all these oats and nut shrapnel off the floor.

I learned a long time ago that popcorn is an amazing snack for when you have a lot of work, and the years I've spent tinkering my proprietary nutritional yeast–heavy spice blend have really paid off. Your fingers get messy and that makes it impossible to type, but it's not because you *can't*

Work-avoidant granola

The stuff of gelatinous stock

write—it's the popcorn's fault. Anyway, it's temporary. By the time the bowl is empty, you'll be raring to go.

I often get stuck a few sentences in, and for that, making a cake is helpful. It keeps me from spiraling—and even without a stand mixer, the toasted sesame batter I've been tinkering with comes together quick. Once the cake is in the oven, I will set a timer and use that interval for uninterrupted writing. Gotta get back to those pages! My word count varies. The amount of sugar-encrusted, tight-crumbed cake the recipe yields is reliably quantifiable, though. The single-layer cake is enriched with toasted sesame oil, which not only makes it smell amazing, but gives it a two- or three-day lifespan, even if held at room temperature on the kitchen counter. Normally that's a good thing, but for me it means I won't be able to use the cake excuse tomorrow.

Sometimes I'll get to the end of the day and realize, wow, I did nothing. Probably my brain needs to recharge. On those days, I like to start a giant pot of stock at night, which is smarter and more interesting than going to bed at a normal hour. Once the bones and vegetable scraps I've been hoarding in the freezer have come to the barest simmer in my tallest pot, I can finally retire.

You know the old saying—*Why write when you can enjoy meat smells wafting through the house all night?* I came up with that one. In the morning, I'll jump right into an essay. But first, I have to drain and strain eight quarts of bone broth, of course, then pick every bit of cartilage and meat off the bones to give to Margie, my sweet doggie, who is waiting right here with her wet nose pressed into my thigh.

When the stock is labeled and cooling down in multiple containers, I wash the pot and the colander and wipe down the counters that have been lightly anointed with animal fat. *Then* I can make coffee and fill my big water bottle, pick out some music, and write.

Alone Popcorn
A huge single portion

Vegetable oil, ideally peanut, for popping

Scant ½ cup popcorn kernels

Extra-virgin olive oil

Kosher salt

Nutritional yeast

Aleppo pepper

Freshly ground black pepper

Granulated garlic

MSG

Place a 5-quart Dutch oven or other heavy pot with a lid over medium-high heat. Add enough vegetable oil to generously coat the surface, then pour in the kernels. If there isn't enough oil to fully lubricate the kernels, add some more. Without enough oil, the heat won't conduct properly, and instead of steam expanding inside the kernel with a force great enough to blow the whole thing open, the kernels will simply char.

Cover the pot and cook until the kernels start to pop. Lower the heat to medium and cook, occasionally lifting up the pot up and giving it a few forceful up-and-down shakes, until the popping slows to every couple of seconds or so.

Turn off the heat and let the popcorn settle for a minute. This is mostly psychological. The most important part is about to begin. I prefer to season the popcorn right in the pot, but if you feel constrained, transfer it to your biggest bowl first. Drizzle in just enough olive oil to lightly coat the popcorn, tossing with a big wooden spoon or spatula all the while. Start slow rather than dousing; a light coating is all that's needed to give the seasonings something to hold onto. Season with a 4-finger pinch of salt and toss to combine. Taste and adjust the salt level. A good amount of popcorn will be consumed during the seasoning process, which is why I call for so much to begin with.

Next, go absolutely wild adding nutritional yeast, an ingredient there can never be too much of on popcorn—or anything else, really. Toss again to combine, taste, adjust, and then season to taste with Aleppo, black pepper, and granulated garlic. Add a couple shakes of MSG and check for balance. I've never once measured this and I'm not about to start now. I use a very light hand with the garlic and you don't need much MSG to make a difference, but I like a lot of black pepper and Aleppo, which magically activates the nutritional yeast and makes this popcorn more delicious than Nacho Cheese Doritos. I know, huge claim. I stand by it.

Transfer the popcorn to a big bowl and enjoy however, wherever, and with whomever you like. When the popcorn is gone, there will likely be a generous amount of seasonings left over. Whatever happens between you and the bottom of that bowl is none of my business.

KING
Granola
Granola

Cherry-Cacao Granola

Makes 2 quarts

3 cups rolled oats (not quick-cooking)

2 cups pistachios, peanuts, or almonds

¼ cup cacao nibs, lightly crushed

½ cup extra-virgin olive oil

½ cup pure maple syrup

2 teaspoons kosher salt

1 cup dried sour cherries

Flaky salt

½ cup coarsely chopped bittersweet chocolate (optional)

Preheat the oven to 350°F.

In a large bowl, combine the oats, pistachios, and cacao nibs. Add the oil, maple syrup, and kosher salt and stir to coat. Scrape the mixture onto a large rimmed baking sheet and spread it out, wall to wall.

Bake until the mixture is fragrant and toasty, about 30 minutes, rotating the sheet back to front halfway through (but not stirring).

Add the cherries to the granola and toss them through. Return to the oven and bake until the oats and nuts are dark golden brown, about 5 minutes more.

Season with flaky salt, then sprinkle the chocolate pieces over, if using. Let sit, undisturbed. The chocolate will soften and spread out while the granola cools; don't stir until it firms up again. Store granola airtight, at room temperature, for up to 3 weeks.

Cabinet Door Masala Chai
Makes about 1 quart

Adapted from Spiros Antonopoulos

1 cinnamon stick

1¼ ounces (40g) coarsely grated fresh ginger

Scant 2 tablespoons (10g) strong black tea, such as Assam

¾ teaspoon (2g) cardamom seeds, coarsely ground

2¾ cups (about 650ml) whole milk or plant-based milk

¼ cup (about 75g) maple syrup

Lightly crush the cinnamon so that it breaks into a few shards. Put the ginger and cinnamon in a medium saucepot and pour 3½ cups (900ml) water over. Bring to a boil over high heat, then lower to a simmer and cook until the aroma of the ginger is less spicy and sweeter than it was at the beginning, and the liquid has reduced by about a third. Turn the heat to very low and add the tea, then the cardamom. Let the tea steep in the hot liquid for a few minutes, then pour in the milk and maple syrup.

Return the liquid to a boil over medium-high heat, standing watch. This is a good opportunity for attentive daydreaming and contemplation. Keep your eyes trained on the surface of the liquid the whole time. No stirring. When the liquid finally hits a boil and threatens to spill over the sides of the pot, cut the heat (if using an alt milk, stop at a bare simmer, otherwise it may curdle). Let the liquid settle down, then bring it back to a boil, stopping it again before it boils over. Repeat a third time, which is how I was taught to do it for maximum lucky energy and other types of magic.

Strain the chai into a teapot or large measuring cup. Drink hot or cold. You can let the leftovers cool down to room temperature, then cover and chill for 1 or 2 days.

Gelatinous Stock for Humans and Dogs

Makes 3 to 4 quarts

5 pounds cartilaginous bones, such as beef neck, chicken feet, and/or pork trotters

Kosher salt

Palmful of dried spices, such as fennel or coriander seed, black or white peppercorns, star anise, and/or dried chiles

A few vegetables, such as carrot, fennel, ginger, galangal, onion, leek, garlic, celery, mushroom scraps, and/or lemongrass

Big handful of fresh herbs, such as parsley, cilantro, and/or thyme

Place the bones in a 6- to 8-quart heavy-bottomed stockpot and cover generously with water. Bring to a boil over high heat (uncovered). When the liquid boils, remove it from the heat, transfer the bones to a colander, and discard the liquid. Rinse out the pot.

Put the blanched bones back in the pot, fill with water nearly to the rim, and bring to a boil again, occasionally skimming the foamy scum that breaks the surface. Lower the heat to maintain the barest simmer—a bubble here and there every second or so. Add a pinch of salt, the spices, your vegetables, and your herbs. Simmer very gently for 2 hours, skimming and occasionally pushing the bones around with a wooden spoon so they don't stick.

Fish out the vegetables from the pot. Continue to not-quite-simmer for 8 to 12 hours. This is an extraction, not a reduction. I like to set this up in the evening and let it go all night.

Not going to lie, you might not sleep great while the stock is on the stove. Your dog, if you have one, may howl plaintively off and on during the night. The beefy flavors may work their way into your dreams. If making the stock during the day, go out for an hour or two at some point, and then come back to experience the smell of your home when you walk in the door.

When the time has passed, the chicken feet will be floppier than the weakest handshake, marrow will threaten to slide straight out of the bone tunnels, and any cartilage that was previously sandwiched between the meat and bones will have melted into loose batter.

Transfer the solids to a colander set in a wide bowl. Strain the stock into a very large bowl or a clean, empty pot, then do the same with any liquid that has collected under the colander. Don't skim off the fat, for the love of all that is good.

Let the stock cool, stirring occasionally, then transfer to smaller containers for storing (chilled for 1 week, or frozen for several months). I use the fat on top for cooking. I also pick the meat and cartilage off the spent bones and give it to Marge, my dog, who loves that very much.

Just Like an Olive Oil Cake, but with Sesame Instead

Makes one 9-inch cake

Vegetable oil, for greasing the pan

12 tablespoons (6 ounces/170g/1½ sticks) cold unsalted butter

2 tablespoons (30g) tahini

2 tablespoons (26g) toasted sesame oil

1 tablespoon (18g) white or yellow miso

2 teaspoons vanilla extract

¾ cup (144g) plus 2 tablespoons (24g) sugar, divided

2 lemons

1 cup (120g) all-purpose flour

⅓ cup (42g) fine almond flour

1 teaspoon (3g) kosher salt

1½ teaspoons (7g) baking powder

½ teaspoon (2g) baking soda

3 large eggs

4 tablespoons (35g) sesame seeds, toasted, divided

Preheat the oven to 375°F. Lightly grease a 9-inch cake pan with vegetable oil and line the bottom with a round of parchment paper.

Cut the butter into tablespoon-size pieces and let them temper while you prep your ingredients. You want the butter to be pliable and cool when it's time to mix the batter. If you cannot bend the butter without it breaking, it is too cold.

In a small bowl, mix together the tahini, sesame oil, miso, vanilla, and ¼ cup (60g) warm water until no lumps of miso remain. Set aside.

In the bowl of stand mixer (or large bowl, if using a hand mixer), put ¾ cup (144g) sugar and grate the zest of both lemons over (about 1 tablespoon). Use your fingers to thoroughly work the zest into the sugar. Add the all-purpose flour, almond flour, salt, baking powder, and baking soda and comb through with your hands to combine and break up any lumps.

Add the butter to the dry ingredients and place the bowl onto the mixer fitted with the paddle (or use a hand mixer). Beat on medium speed; the butter will go from chunky to pebbly to sandy, and then the mixture will ball up around the beaters. When that happens, continue beating until the mixture is smooth and some of the batter sticks to the sides of the bowl, another minute or so. Scrape down the bowl and paddle.

Add the eggs one at a time on medium speed, waiting until each is incorporated into the batter and scraping down the bowl before adding the next. (So: add, beat, scrape, repeat.) Stream in the tahini mixture and beat until the batter is emulsified and creamy, 1 or 2 minutes. Remove the bowl from the stand, add 2 tablespoons toasted sesame seeds, and use a rubber spatula to give the batter a few swift mixes, making sure to get all the way to the bottom of the bowl, where sneaky clumps of batter like to hide out.

Scrape the batter into the cake pan and smooth the top. Sprinkle the remaining 2 tablespoons sesame seeds over, then the remaining 2 tablespoons sugar.

Bake the cake until it is dark brown, firm but a tiny bit springy in the center, and starting to pull away from the edge of the pan, 45 to 50 minutes. If you have a digital thermometer, the temperature should be between 205° and 210°F in the center of the cake.

Let cool in the pan for 5 or 10 minutes, then run a paring knife around the edge of the cake to prevent it from sticking. Let cool in the pan 20 minutes more, then carefully invert to release the cake. Peel off the parchment. Cool the cake on a rack, sugared-side up.

This cake is light and fluffy on day one. Lovely. Or, wrap it in wax paper and store at room temperature. On days two and three the cake will have settled down a bit; what it loses in etherealness, it gains in heft and humidity. I like it better once it has rested; you might value loftiness.

Not to overcomplicate things, but you can also slice the cake and then freeze it, airtight, for several months. Thaw, toast, and assess. So many options. The beauty is that you can have this cake and eat it, too. Enjoy a slice several days in a row and decide in the moment when you think it has peaked. It is, after all, your cake we're talking about.

Fancy-Ass Sandwich

On Fridays at Montrachet, we had a shift break between lunch and dinner. It was condoned but not expressly permitted to eat leftover rolls and mini baguettes from the bread warmer, along with cheeses from the cheese board.

My VIP treat was a baguette, spread lusciously on both sides with the European-style butter we kept in 3-pound portions on our stations. I'd add a thick slice of blue cheese from a wedge on the cheese board—Fourme d'Ambert, which I'd never tasted until I worked there. It's semi-firm but very creamy; sharp and tangy without being stinky; sweet from cow's milk and salty from those inoculated pockets of blue. Butter mellowed its sour notes even more.

Once I'd smashed the cheese onto my buttery, torn-open baguette, I topped it with cracked black pepper, like you would a proper wedge salad. If the weather was nice, I'd eat my superior sandwich outside. In a sweaty, 14-hour day, this was a fleeting yet boutique moment for myself.

One Friday, I strolled halfway up the block and parked my booty on a shallow stoop, leaning against the front door of a midcentury brownstone. I didn't have a cell phone. I was sitting there, eating and people-watching, when I noticed an older man walking toward me. In my head he's wearing brown corduroy pants and a blue shirt and carrying a cane and a newspaper, but that could be made up. What's true is that he had real old-school Tribeca energy.

He looked at me in my chef's whites gnawing on a baguette, and I looked at him right back. As he passed, he said, with a whiff of irony "*Bon appétit,* Chef." I raised my half-eaten sandwich in a mini salute. In that moment, something passed between us. I knew he was the kind of person who would eat at Montrachet, and he knew I'd be cooking on the other side of those swinging kitchen doors. In our sidewalk meet-up, the veil was lifted. Inside, I prepare foie gras for the rich New Yorkers, but out here, I make my own feast.

It's one of my most treasured memories.

Sometimes the craving for blue cheese with butter and black pepper leaps from my core and consumes me, and when that happens, I satisfy it.

An unimpeachable combination

Buttered Crackers with Blue Cheese and Pepper
For 1 or more

Room-temperature butter

Crackers, they better be salted

Fourme d'Ambert or any other blue cheese that you like

Freshly cracked pepper

The only problem with this snack is that it is not ready on demand. The butter and the cheese need to be at room temperature. You can get around cold butter by shaving it into thin planks with a vegetable peeler and then transferring the strips onto the cracker. Cold cheese, however, is the wrong texture and temperature. It won't move on the cracker properly or taste as good. Plan ahead.

When it's time, butter a cracker. (If you happen to have a warm baguette around, by all means, use that!) Add a robust schmear of blue cheese. Season well with cracked pepper. Repeat as needed.

To share this snack in a party atmosphere, put out a board with the cheese, the butter, the crackers, a few butter knives, and a pepper mill, and tell everyone what to do.

Sleep, Routine, Protein

In the summer of 2017, I decided to invest in a few sessions with a personal trainer—nothing crazy—five, maybe ten max. Since then, I've followed that same coach to eight different gyms and counting, and discovered how good it feels to be strong.

Gym selfie

The person encouraging me to pick up heavy things is Ross Twanmoh, one of the finest examples of man concentrate you'll ever see ("short king" is so cliché). I'd taken his debilitating "Ropes and Rowers" classes at the gym, where his energy did not seem to align with the reigning crowd of cheerful fitness Muppets. He was all business, no platitudes. He could reduce a roomful of adults to a panting pile of overexercised puppies, then lead us through breathwork that reset our nervous systems. He wore soccer shoes and a full sleeve of tattoos, talked about joint mobility, and could no doubt hoist a Jeep over his head if necessary. I could tell he loathed the pop-star headset-mic thing he had to wear, which endeared me to him even more.

The gym wouldn't let me contact Ross directly for one-on-one sessions, so I did what any normal woman in her mid-forties would do: slid into his DMs and badgered him until we had an appointment. Since then, no amount of sessions has been enough. Ross taught me how to use barbells, kettlebells, and dumbbells. Once a week, he makes me do deadlifts, chest presses, curls, walking lunges, back lunges, forward lunges, snatches, and cleans. Plus, the squats: back squats, front squats, goblet squats, sumo squats, rear-foot elevated split squats. He makes me slam medicine balls into the floor and stagger across the room clutching 70-pound sandbags to my torso, and I punish him by telling him it made me pee a little. On the days I don't see him, I have his written instructions and I work out on my own. I generally hate going, but I love when the workouts are done. If I keep it up, maybe someday I will kinda-sorta want to go.

My physical transformations don't align with trite before-and-afters, and I stopped weighing myself a long time ago. I have callouses on my palms from gripping the barbell and bruises on my thighs from resting weights there between sets. When I noticed some shirt sleeves getting tighter, I accepted it, knowing muscle was changing the shape of my arm. Within a year of strength training, my decades-long back pain receded, which amazed me, and it creeps back if I slack off. I care less and less about

Angels

what my body looks like, and am more attached to what it can do. It's easy to track progress when it can be measured in kilos.

Ross is one inch taller than me, and that's where the physical similarities end. He's pure muscle and I'm a mix of a lot of things, including full-fat yogurt and copious amounts of olive oil. Our body shapes reflect our priorities in life, and our jobs. The reason I'm not more muscular, according to Ross, is because of one thing: protein. Recently he said: *Essentially, all the work you've done over the past eight years is moot because you don't eat enough protein.*

The statement didn't make me wither. It's classic motivational speech coming from Ross. Deadpan-flat is his main inspirational tone. The others are curt-directive, as in *Let's go!* when I'm attempting a challenging rep, and sarcastic-dismissive, as in *But, are you dead?* when I complain. Humor is my first line of defense against any sensation of pain—be it physical or emotional. My motivation is to try to make Ross laugh while he's torturing me, and his task is to try to make me stronger despite my relentless attempts to distract him. We make a dynamic team.

I'm constantly promising that I'm going to go to the gym on certain days, and that I'm going to go to sleep earlier, and that I'm going to eat more protein. I am really good at not doing those things. This is called striving. And yet, I keep showing up for our weekly hangs, at least five minutes late, like clockwork. Over the years I've learned that just because I could do something last week doesn't mean I'll be able to repeat it this week. A miss last week could return as a win next month. This nonlinear progress has emerged in other areas of my life, from my work to my moods. Rather than spiraling from small frustrations, I sometimes catch myself muttering *Let's go* under my breath.

If I send Ross a photo of what I'm eating, like my favorite sweet potatoes with black vinegar, chili crisp, with a little dollop of yogurt, he will write back: *Where's the protein?* Deadpan-flat. But if I tell him I made myself a protein smoothie before the gym, or that I figured out a way to make cottage cheese delicious even for people who hate cottage cheese, or that I developed a pasta with both canned tuna *and* a jammy egg for extra heft, he'll congratulate me—in his way.

That's a good amount of protein, but would it kill *you to try it with tuna packed in water?*

Actually, if I don't use tuna packed in oil, I might die.

If I've learned anything from this relationship, it's that I can use sarcastic-dismissive, too.

Once in a while, I will hit a new PR when Ross and I are together—a 200-pound deadlift, a set of box jump-overs where I don't fall flat on my ass, my heaviest kettlebell swing yet. On those days, Ross will applaud me with one word: *Olé!* It feels amazing.

A couple of sessions later, though, he'll be adding more weights to the bar, or more reps to the set, and we're right back where I started: struggling.

Great, now I can't do it, I say.

He looks at me: *You know this isn't ever supposed to be easy, right?*

Right. And now I know: I can do more. Even when I can't.

Mac offers support after dreaded box jumps

Tuna Pasta for People Who Don't Count Macros
2 generous servings

¼ cup extra-virgin olive oil

1 small red onion, thinly sliced

Kosher salt; freshly ground black pepper

3 anchovy fillets, drained

4 garlic cloves, thinly sliced

½ teaspoon crushed red pepper flakes

1 tablespoon capers, drained (rinsed if salted)

2 large eggs

10 ounces mezzi rigatoni pasta

2 (6.7-ounce) jars tuna packed in oil, drained

½ lemon

Handful of flat-leaf parsley, roughly chopped

Bring a large pot of salted water to boil. Fill a medium bowl with ice water.

While you're waiting for the water to boil, heat a 12-inch skillet or medium Dutch oven over medium until hot. Add the olive oil and onion. Season with salt and black pepper and cook, stirring frequently, until the onions start to soften, about 2 minutes. Cover and cook the onions, stirring occasionally, until they are completely soft but haven't taken on any color, 6 to 10 minutes (lower the heat as needed if the onions start browning).

Add the anchovies, garlic, and pepper flakes and cook, stirring, until the anchovy disintegrates and the garlic and onion are golden, about 3 minutes. Add the capers and cook until they start to fry in the oil, 1 or 2 minutes. The onions will take on color, but don't let them burn. Cover the sauce and remove from the heat until the pasta is ready.

Boil the eggs for 7 minutes for jammy yolks. Cool in the ice water. In the same pot of water, cook the pasta until very al dente, 2 to 3 minutes less than the package instructions. While the pasta is cooking, gently peel the eggs and set them aside.

Use a spider to transfer the pasta to the onion mixture in the skillet. (Alternately, reserve about 1½ cups pasta liquid, then drain the pasta in a colander.) Return to medium heat. Toss the pasta with the onion mixture, adding pasta water as needed, until the pasta is generously coated with sauce. Add the tuna and squeeze in the juice of the lemon half. Cook, tossing, until the pasta is done and the tuna is distributed through the sauce and warmed through, 2 to 3 minutes. Try not to mash up the tuna too much; there should still be visible pieces.

Toss the parsley into the pasta. Divide the pasta between two bowls and top each with an egg and a few extra grinds of black pepper.

Protein-Peanut Butter-Banana-Blueberry-Coffee (PPBBBC) Smoothie

Makes 2 smoothies

1½ cups plant-based or cow's milk

1 shot espresso or ½ cup cold coffee

1 scoop chocolate or unflavored protein powder

1 fresh or frozen banana

½ cup frozen blueberries

2 tablespoons peanut butter

Kosher salt

Ice

Maple syrup, agave, or honey

In a blender, combine the milk, espresso, and protein powder and blend on low speed to break up the protein powder and prevent it from clumping. Add the banana, berries, peanut butter, a pinch of salt, and a big handful of ice cubes. (If you're using frozen banana, do a smaller handful of ice.) Blend on high speed until the smoothie is thick and smooth and forms a vortex in the blender jar. If it's too thick and won't catch, add a splash of water or additional milk. If too thin, add more ice and continue to blend. Taste and sweeten as desired with maple syrup.

Turkish Cottage Cheese Egg

Serves 1

5 ounces cottage cheese

¼ cup Greek yogurt

Extra-virgin olive oil, for drizzling

Kosher salt

2 tablespoons unsalted butter

1 garlic clove, smashed

¼ cup chopped walnuts

Small handful of dill, thinly sliced (about ¼ cup)

1 teaspoon Aleppo pepper, plus more for seasoning

1 or 2 large eggs

Flaky salt

Toast or pita chips, for serving

In a small bowl, combine the cottage cheese and yogurt and add a drizzle of oil. Whisk until very well combined. If you prefer no texture, use an immersion blender. Taste cottage cheese and season with kosher salt. Spoon the mixture into a shallow serving bowl and use the back of a spoon to spread it out and create a well in the center; this is the landing pad for your egg.

Place a small skillet over medium heat. Add the butter and garlic and cook, stirring, until the butter is foaming, about 2 minutes. Add the walnuts and a pinch of kosher salt. Cook, stirring, until the butter has browned and the walnuts are toasted, 2 to 4 minutes more. Off heat, add the dill and Aleppo and stir until the sizzling stops. Set the skillet aside.

Meanwhile, bring a small saucepan of water to a simmer. Lower the heat until only the tiniest of bubbles are breaking the surface. Crack an egg into a small bowl, then gently tilt the egg into the water. Let cook, undisturbed, until you see the whites start to set, about 20 seconds. Gently stir the water to get the egg to start spinning on itself, then cover the pot and turn off the heat. For a gently poached egg with a runny yolk, cook 3 minutes. (If cooking 2 eggs, add the second one after the first one has been cooking for about 20 seconds, then repeat the waiting and stirring process.) Lift up the egg(s) with a slotted spoon and blot off excess liquid on a kitchen towel.

Place the egg(s) into the dairy divot and season with flaky salt and Aleppo. Spoon the brown butter/walnut sauce over the egg(s) and onto the cottage cheese and drizzle with a little extra oil. Serve with toast.

Steamed and Crispy Sweet Potatoes
For 1

2 Japanese sweet potatoes (about 6 ounces each)

Kosher salt

1 tablespoon extra-virgin olive oil

¼ cup labne

2 teaspoons black vinegar

Chili crisp and flaky salt, for serving

Bring a few inches of water to a simmer in a medium pot fitted with a steamer basket. Scrub the sweet potatoes, then steam until completely tender all the way through, 35 to 40 minutes. Set aside until cool enough to handle.

> **Get ahead:** The sweet potatoes can be refrigerated for up to 5 days. Cool completely, then cover and chill. Scale this recipe up and steam several at a time for meal-prepping, if desired.

Slice the potatoes crosswise into ¾-inch-thick pieces. Season all over with kosher salt. Preheat a heavy-bottomed skillet over medium-high for a couple of minutes, then add the oil. Arrange the sweet potato slices in a single layer. Cook until undersides are dark brown and caramelized, 2 to 3 minutes. Turn and cook until second side is similarly browned, 2 to 3 minutes more. Transfer to a serving plate.

Spoon labne onto the plate and use the curved side of the spoon to create a divot. Drizzle with the black vinegar and spoon some chili crisp onto the yogurt and over the potatoes. Season with flaky salt.

Things I Tell Myself When I Feel Out of Sorts

Be cringe. Be rare. Take risks. Fail. Don't talk yourself out of it. Don't be afraid to be unliked. Don't forget to cry. Read books in bed. Sit in front of fires. Take pictures of the moon, even though they're never good. Send people your bad pictures of the moon. Breathe so your belly rises. Commune with animals. Notice envy. Notice jealousy. Be creative. Be honest. Be upfront. Be truthful. Be safe for other people. Wish less. Don't spend time with people who make you feel stupid. Work with people you love. Take money from corporations. Trust your work. Trust the vibes. Believe that you have value. Your age is neither good nor bad. Be physically strong. Be in hotness. Don't wear uncomfortable underwear. Don't run red lights. Courtesy wave. Be consistent. Be trustworthy. Be more funny. Be loved. Love.

6. Warmer Days

speaker
candles
lights
shower
get dressed
flower station
plates/glasses
silver/napkins
celery
toast
aioli
light fire
BAR lemons mixers limes ice cups
mix olives/almonds
bring lamb out
slice bread
outside clean
outside kitchen
Italian Folk Magic
Rue's Kitchen Witchery

LAMB
/31/25
LINED
VERTAMAE
SMART-GROSVEN
VIBRATI
COOKIN
OR, THE TRAVEL N
A GEECHE
TUESDAY
2/11
Write: Reasons/chips
Convert 2 Recipes
Pleasure not
Live 55 vids
2025/365

Revisionist Sundays

Before the separation, I made pasta e fagioli almost every Sunday, year-round. Even with the little alterations I brought to it weekly, the cooking and consuming of it was grounding, pleasing, and reliable—all the things traditions are made of.

When it became just me and Cosmo on our alternating weekends, fazool no longer felt right. His brother was at college, and it was a hard dish to make for two people—not just because of the generous serving size. The recipe was deeply interwoven with the rhythm of a different family dynamic, one that was in the past. Serving it would have felt like shining a spotlight on what wasn't there.

But let us not throw the baby out with the bean water. At the time, I had an increasingly independent social teenager whom I was invested in reeling back in for Sunday dinner. I wanted to have a new tradition to go with our new life, something steady to mirror the role that soup had played. I hatched a plan for us to cook a new dish—together—every week. We'd pick out a recipe a few days ahead, I'd take care of the shopping, and then we'd convene in the kitchen, elbow-to-elbow, two little line cooks. I pitched it to Coz, who loves cheffing it up, and he was in. I thought this would be a great way to give him the foundation of a cook's canon, and obviously the potential for bonding was huge. He'd remember these Sundays with Mom when he got older, I just knew it.

We did this new thing exactly once. On our kickoff Sunday in the fall, we made pasta with Bolognese sauce. It was fun, too. We read through recipes from Missy Robbins, Marcella Hazan, and Giuliano Bugialli and decided to riff. We compared ratios of ground meat and vegetables for the soffritto and debated the inclusion of milk, stock, nutmeg, and tomato paste. We chose, wisely, not to make pasta from scratch.

I let Cosmo do most of the hands-on cooking while I darted around, opening wine, locating the bay leaves, putting a measuring cup under his nose for the milk. I'm very comfortable in this role, having undergone years of training as the locator of Lego pieces during ambitious builds. It was all very "I'll hold your purse while you're on the red carpet," but I don't mind being the sous-chef.

Dinner was delish. Pork and beef, reduced to a sublime sludge, buried in Parm. We both had seconds, and he took the leftovers to school for lunch. Two weeks later, when it was time to choose a new recipe, Cosmo suggested we make Bolognese again. I wasn't in a meaty mood, though, and he wasn't too enthused about flipping through cookbooks. Forcing the thing wasn't the right vibe. I remember sitting on the sofa doing work stuff on my computer that afternoon while he played video games on the TV, both of us content. I roasted a chicken for dinner instead, which we ate together, and without an announcement or much in the way of acknowledgment, our Sunday supper collab came to an end. The next time, I made fusilli with broccoli and lemony bread crumbs. The one after that, we went out for ramen. We both loved our chill Sunday dinners, even when we weren't the ones doing the cooking. Being together was enough.

Cosmo and I found our Sunday dinner groove and leaned into the uncertainty of what it would be. The tradition now is simply that Sunday dinner is a joint activity, and we achieve that consistently without needing a recipe-research-and-shopping assignment. The meal is determined by our moods, a craving one of us is having, the amount of time we feel like committing to cooking, which market I happen to pass by on the way back from the gym.

I have a deep appreciation for the kinds of things I can do when I don't have to spend three hours making soup, like lying on my bed and not worrying about whether the beans are done. If Cosmo is out with friends, there's a chance they'll come back for dinner at ours. There are nights we cook together or split tasks—he's gotten really skilled at making steaks, less great at wiping down splatter. Together, we've become creatures of a shared, unfettered, and freewheeling habit, letting Sundays sort themselves out. And when we're feeling extravagant, we have a really solid recipe for Bolognese: it's ours.

If You Make One Bolognese . . .
Makes 6 cups, enough for 8 servings

3 garlic cloves

2 celery stalks

1 medium carrot

1 medium yellow onion

½ fennel bulb

⅓ cup extra-virgin olive oil, plus more for serving

4 ounces pancetta, diced

Kosher salt; freshly ground pepper

1 pound ground beef

1 pound ground pork

2 tablespoons tomato paste

½ cup whole milk

3 bay leaves

1 cup white wine

1 to 2 pounds fettuccine or rigatoni

Parmigiano, for serving

Roughly chop the garlic, celery, carrot, onion, and fennel, then transfer to a food processor and pulse until finely chopped, scraping down the bowl as needed.

Heat ⅓ cup oil and the pancetta in a large Dutch oven over medium. Cook until most of the fat has rendered and the pancetta is turning golden brown. Add the vegetables, stir to coat, and season with salt and pepper. Cover and cook, stirring occasionally, until the soffritto is juicy and has lost about a third of its volume, 10 minutes.

Add both types of ground meat and stir to combine. Cook, stirring occasionally, until the meats are no longer pink, about 10 minutes. Stir in the tomato paste and cook until it has turned a deeper shade of red, about 5 minutes. Pour in the milk, add the bay leaves, and increase the heat to bring the liquid to a simmer. Cook, stirring occasionally, until the milk has almost completely evaporated, about 15 minutes.

Add the wine, return to a simmer, partially cover, and cook until the meat is extremely tender, and the sauce has reduced by about half and feels velvety, about 3 hours. Check and stir occasionally, and loosen the sauce with water as needed.

Get ahead: Transfer the Bolognese to a container, let cool, then refrigerate for up to 1 week, or freeze for up to 3 months.

Bring a large pot of generously salted water to a boil. For every 4 people, use 1 pound of pasta and 3 cups sauce. Scale up or down from there.

Cook the pasta until very al dente, a few minutes less than the package instructions. Transfer the pasta to the pot with the sauce along with about 1 cup pasta cooking liquid. Simmer the pasta in the sauce, gently stirring and tossing occasionally, until the pasta is al dente. Serve with Parmigiano for grating over.

RECYCLE
ME

Sand, Sun, and Stone Fruit

It was a Saturday in July, fourteen months into my life as a single person. Because I can do whatever I want, I decided to drive to the beach.

My favorite spot is a fifteen-minute trek from the western end of the Jacob Riis parking lot, down an overgrown side road I like to call the Portal of Transition, beyond which is a secluded section bordered by grassy dunes. There, I can lean into the ease of being alone, which is not the same as loneliness. Beaching alone, eating alone at the bar, going to the movies alone: This is a joy. It's taken being a grown-up to fully melt into that.

I lowered my towel onto the sand a respectable distance away from an enviably tanned couple, a small group under a flowy direct-to-consumer sun umbrella, and some topless women sharing a joint. Memories of past beach days with my then-husband and my boys started percolating, and rather than batting them away, I tried to let those happy moments replay without letting it undermine my pleasure in the present. I want to believe it's possible to treasure both.

Before getting too comfortable, I forced myself into the chilly water. This feels like an errand; it simply must be done. I don't want to be the procrastinator of yore, the younger mom who would stall knee-deep in the surf while my children hollered at me to *Just get in!* I waited a long time for the life I have now, and I'm done with delays. I submerged myself quickly, let out a little squeal, then floated around long enough to confirm it didn't *feel* as bad as 66°F *sounded*. As I walked back to my towel, dripping, the air felt warm on my skin.

I had a few things to nosh on and a pile of reading material, two beverages, and nowhere to be. I got into the peaches first. I can't eat a peach without remembering being in my third trimester with Cosmo, fourteen summers prior, an amazing season for stone fruit. I'd buy seven yellow peaches on Saturdays, in various degrees of ripeness, then eat one a day until the weekend rolled around again. This became a late-pregnancy fixation, a reliable delight when every part of my body, from my puffy feet to my acid reflux, was otherwise compromised.

CLOVER FARMS DAIRY
CALIFORNIA TREE FRUIT FROM FAMILY FARMS
SUMMERTIME

My pint container of beach peaches reflected the range I found languishing on my counter that morning. Quite the medley. There were a couple with bruises. One peach had started to mold, a sprinkle of green baby powder at the pointed end. A perfect one in the mix, too. I trimmed what I could, and cut each into pieces.

Eating them all mixed up was like sampling every phase in a peach's life cycle. The best bites were creamy and juicy and tasted like honey and almonds, cherry juice, Creamsicle. The wedges with bruises were stringy in some parts, semi-liquid in others. Another piece was a tiny bit bubbly on my tongue; a hint of fermentation, not yet spoiled. The overripe flavor in others was sweet-and-sour, like brown sugar and vinegar mother. I liked some more than others. I ate them all. I wished I had salt for the sweetest ones, or a squeeze of lime for the funky ones. I settled for salty skin, licking sea water from my upper lip.

I finished the peaches and ditched my bikini top, feeling uninhibited. I relish the relatively tame exhibitionism of exposing my boobs. Always have. I stretched out on my back, propped my head on my beach bag, and pulled my baseball cap down low. With tits out, sun on my chest and arms, water evaporating on my thighs, lingering peach juice in my mouth, I breathed deeply. I watched my stomach rise, and I let my midsection distend, sunny-side up. I unbuckled the self-imposed, imaginary cinch that is always trying to contain my tummy roll. I didn't care how it looked—not here, not today—and was sure none of my seaside neighbors did either.

When I exhaled, I finally, truly relaxed. *You're not an overripe peach,* I tell myself. I am neither peak, nor post-peak, nor in decline. My younger self didn't have more potential than I do now. Mothering babies isn't more meaningful than parenting teens, and what it feels like to be unmarried will continue to morph over time. It's not better to share; it's not worse to keep the best bits for yourself. I'm alone, half-naked, and my stomach is soft. The water is cold, and the waves are gentle. Everything is mixed: sour and sweet, tart and mushy. Everything is worth having.

Maybe the variability and the uncertainty create desire. If I thought I'd already had the best peach of my life, I'd never eat another. I've got to believe there's a better one—a peach, a lover, a hair day—that will exceed any that came before. Even if I were handed the certified most ambrosial peach ever to exist in the history of peaches, I'd want to try it with a wee pinch of salt—maybe it will reach new heights! Who can say!

I felt wiser for peaching, happy I ate the weird ones, amused by my fruit philosophizing. I raised myself up on my elbows to survey the scene. Plenty of day left. I was already plotting my return to the water for a second dip, knowing it would be even easier to get in this time, and that the pleasure of warm air on my skin afterward was guaranteed.

The actual day and the actual peaches

Beach Peaches
Serves 1

High-summer peaches, as many as you want

1 fat lime wedge and flaky salt, if you're fancy

Cut away any soft spots or bruises from the peaches, if necessary. Cut into 4 or 6 wedges each. Remove the skin with a paring knife, or don't. Transfer to an airtight container and chill overnight, or for however long you can.

Go to the beach with the peaches, a pair of chopsticks or a fork, with or without the lime and the salt. Squeeze some lime juice over the peaches and season with salt before eating or have them plain. Sometimes the salt left on your upper lip after swimming is enough.

Equinox Party

In March 2025, shortly before this book was due, I decided to stop everything and throw a party to celebrate the spring equinox.

Winter is not my season. I'm a high-summer August baby, a full-on beach freak, salt-hair and frozen-grape kind of girl. The year I wrote this book, I was especially taken by spring's diva-ish themes of rebirth, renewal, and resurrection. It felt important to mark the return of imperceptibly longer days with a backyard party.

A highly specific vision revealed itself to me: a big gathering on a warm early spring night, with a feast I'd cook in my outdoor fireplace, which is where my culinary powers peak. I secured the date and started planning the menu for a couple dozen friends who'd stuck with me through my divorce and the subsequent stitching back together.

Coming up with the dishes was weirdly easy. There would be spiced and rolled lamb breast cooked like porchetta (which I'd never made, but it sure sounded good). I had an idea for an aioli laced with fennel, coriander, mustard seeds, and mint to complement the smoky lamb. Something sharp and spicy would be a nice relief against that fatty richness; I liked the sound of pickled onions and fresh chiles. That in turn begged for something cool and crunchy to put out the fire, so I added a shaved vegetable salad and started concepting a nutty, anchovy-laced dressing. The goal was for everything to taste good when it mingled and meshed, which was inevitable since my friends would be standing outside eating off of melamine plates. I could even see the elements working together as an open-faced sandwich, and added crusty bread to the lineup. I'd warm it in the fire.

I surprised myself by securing the boneless lamb shoulders two days ahead. I came up with a dried spice mix, seasoned the lamb thoroughly on all sides, then tied them (imperfectly) and set them in the fridge to become one with the seasonings. I wrote a shopping list, a day-before prep list, a day-of prep list, and tallied my roster of RSVP yes-es. Look at how organized and on top of it she is! Almost like she does this for a living.

The night before the party, I put the lamb in a very low oven to cook while I slept. And slept I did—in fact, I woke up later than I should have, and went to the gym anyway. Taking that moment of self-care would eat

Scenes from my very frantic slicing

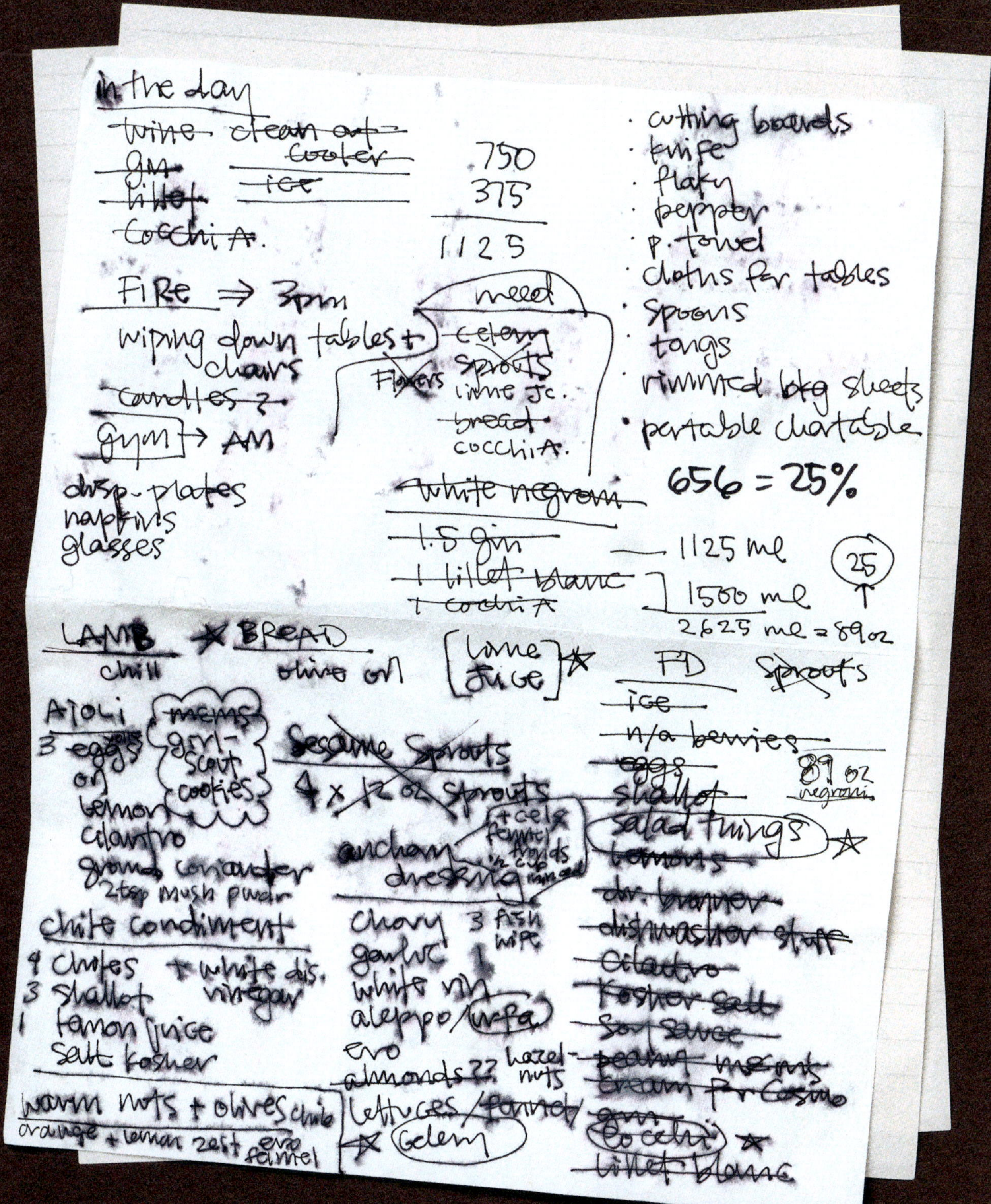
in the day
wine
clean out cooler
gin
ice
lillet
Cocchi A.
750
375
1125
FIRE ⇒ 3pm
wiping down tables + chairs
candles ?
gym → AM
need
celery
Flowers
sprouts
lime jc.
bread
COCCHI A.
cutting boards
knife
flaky
pepper
p. towel
cloths for tables
spoons
tongs
rimmed bkg sheets
portable chartable
disp. plates
napkins
glasses
white negroni
1.5 gin
1 lillet blanc
1 cocchi A
1125 ml
1500 ml
2625 ml = 89 oz
656 = 25%
25
LAMB
chill
BREAD
olive oil
lime juice
FD
sprouts
ice
n/a berries
eggs
shallot
salad things
lemons
dr. bronner
dishwasher stuff
cilantro
kosher salt
soy sauce
cream for Cosmo
gin
Cocchi
lillet blanc
89 oz negroni
AIOLI
3 eggs yolks
oil
lemon
cilantro
ground coriander
2 tsp mush pwdr
moms
girl-scout cookies
Sesame Sprouts
4 x 12 oz sprouts
+ celery fennel fronds
anchovy dressing
chovy
3 fish
garlic
white vin
aleppo
evo
almonds ??
hazel-nuts
lettuces / fennel
celery
chile condiment
4 chiles
3 shallot
1 lemon juice
salt kosher
+ white dis. vinegar
warm nuts + olives
chile
orange + lemon zest
evo
fennel

into the limited time I'd set aside for prep, but I had this on lock. The lamb was done—there were just some salad-y things left to do. Right? Riiiiiight.

By the time I got back from the gym, it was 2 p.m. I was, as the kids say, in the shits. This wasn't as bad as the night of my ill-fated onion soubise at Union Pacific, but the familiar mix of panic and frenzy that fueled me as a line cook was creeping into my chest. I went straight out back in my gross gym clothes to light the fire and started schlepping kitchen equipment up and down the tight spiral staircase that leads to my yard: my cutting board and knives, ingredients for the salad and the pickled onions, olive oil, salt and pepper, tongs and spoons, prep bowls, water bottle, and my portable speaker. It was gorgeous out, and it was now 3 p.m.

My favorite mortar and pestle, now broken beyond repair

I kept repeating *I am just one person* to myself. It was part mantra, part reassurance, part prayer. Once I got going, the mania worked in my favor: The fennel and celery flew through the mandoline blades, creating chic V-shaped shavings. I scooped them into a bowl of ice water to prevent them from oxidizing and kept cranking.

The onions and chiles looked so pretty together as I tossed them with big pinches of kosher salt, red and white rings that mingled with lemon juice and vinegar to exude a psychedelic-pink liquid. I'd come up with this condiment to go with some black beans and rice I made for my older child, Leo, a while back—a throw-together condiment we both added to our bowls until there was none left. The party was an opportunity to work on it a bit more, turn it into a real recipe.

The one thing missing from all of my cute checklists was help. There she is again, the stubborn toddler: *I can do it myself!* But I'd forgotten about the tasks I counted on my ex and the boys to take care of on previous party days—picking up bagged ice and setting up the cooler; wiping down the outdoor tables; carting the plates, cups, and silverware out back. Oh well. I was just one person, but I'd figure it out.

By the time I was hand-whisking the aioli, I was again in control. I felt my heart rate drop as I whisked a trickle of oil into the egg yolks and lemon juice until they were opaque and glossy, as I'd been taught during the first week of culinary school. Knowing the emulsion was set, I tilted the measuring cup and widened the stream. The weight of the cup lightened in my left hand, and the resistance increased for the right hand moving the whisk, physical feedback that corresponded to the magic trick happening before my eyes. Cooking. So cool.

The main elements of the meal were done, and I relished the dopamine hit of crossing each one off the list. Next it was off to the corner wine store for the gin and Cocchi I needed to make a big batch of serve-yourself Negronis. Ross, a former barback, had given me the idea, and his ratios, so I'd name the drink for him. I upended entire bottles of vermouth and Cocchi over a punch bowl and spun them to create a vortex that sucked out the liquid, just like we used to do at Montrachet when making wine reductions.

While in the kitchen, I threw a bag of soybean sprouts into boiling water for a couple of minutes to soften them, then tossed them with a mix of ingredients I also use for edamame—sesame oil, soy sauce, black pepper, and gochugaru. It was a departure from the otherwise Med-inspired menu, but I had no doubt the flavors would pair with the spices in the lamb and the aioli. I'd strategically left dessert off my menu. Instead of baking, I dumped party-size bags of peanut M&M's into tall glass jars and lined up the Girl Scout cookies that my niece, Gia, had hand-delivered the weekend before.

Did I get into the shower twenty minutes before call time? Yes. Was my hair wet and makeup half-done when the doorbell rang? Also yes. Did I have party pants on, though? Thrillingly, yes. Rather than offering drinks, I assigned last-minute jobs to the first six people who walked in the door. Andrew cut lemon and lime wedges for the bar, and Ben took care of the ice bucket. My sister, Nina, took the plates and cups I handed down from the extra-high shelf where we keep that stuff. Where I keep that stuff.

Whenever anyone asked what they could bring, I'd told them I'd happily take bodega flowers—it matched the spring theme. Sweet Kelsey helped shuttle water-filled vases and shears to the dining room table. Whoever brought bouquets could take care of getting them into water, a task loathed by party hosts around the world.

Soon, my special helpers had Swole Negronis in their hands, and we went down to the garden. The lamb was warming up next to the coals in the fireplace, along with a cast-iron skillet with olives, citrus peels, and crushed spices. I'd pulled it off.

Or had I? Within 15 minutes, it started to rain. Rain is such a strong word—I prefer to call it a steady drizzle. *It's not raining!* I hollered up the stairs as the new arrivals stuck their heads out on the deck to say hi. I sought backup from the fireplace gang, all of us busily ignoring the droplets splashing in our cups: *Just a spring mist, right?* But there was no convincing the other half of the party to venture beyond the living room.

I held off for as long as I could, waiting for my party vision to rematerialize. We were supposed to be outside, by the fire, under the dark new-moon sky, celebrating earthly transitions! I texted the person I'd been dating for a few months—he was out of town and had sweetly been checking in on my progress throughout the day. I told him it was fully raining and he wrote back, *Sometimes when we celebrate mother Gaia, she shows herself.*

A beautiful, comforting mess

He was being cute, but he had a point. With that, I abdicated to the ancestral goddess and put out the call to move it inside. As quickly as friends had helped me bring all that stuff out, they reappeared to haul it back in. My sister arranged a buffet on the kitchen counter, and my cook friends, Alivia and Amelia, dressed the salad while I sliced the lamb. We popped the bread into the oven instead of warming it by the fire, and transferred the aioli and the pickled onions to little bowls. Vibrations were high: Negronis were flowing, and a few of us may have even indulged in some magic mushrooms—in honor of Mother Earth, of course.

Once everyone had filled their plates, I clinked a glass to make a toast. *Welcome, my sweet bunnies and forest fairies,* I started.

We're emerging from the darkest days of winter, and I brought you here to celebrate the end of our hibernation. I looked into the faces of my friends, who knew exactly which dark days I was referring to. I told them the sun was coming back, and having their love was the same warmth for me. *The thing about spring is that it always comes back, you just have to wait. No matter what goes down, if we have each other, we'll come out the other side.* One or two people teared up, but I kept it together.

The rain didn't ruin the party. It was a blessing. It pushed my friends into the kitchen and living room, where I saw them sitting three-to-a-loveseat and sharing dining room chairs. There was a whole crew doing stand-up dinner in the kitchen, and when the platters of lamb ran low, they sliced more without needing to ask. Most of us didn't even have forks; they'd been forgotten in the outside set-up, and no one seemed to care. I watched as people from all aspects of my life met each other, and heard myself repeating *Wait, you guys never met before??* Ross connected with Roddy and Joey; Fran was in deep cahoots with Omega and Danni. Natalie was bonding with my sister.

Everything I want most in life was happening, everyone chatting and eating my food with their hands, dipping lamb into aioli and squishing torn pieces of warm bread into the vinaigrette in the salad bowl. They were thrilled when I came around with the jar of M&M's and let me pour candy into their cupped palms.

When the party started to thin out, I clung to my friends and told them they could never leave, but one by one, they did. I was barefoot when the last ones took off, and waved them off from my front step, laughing as they made their way down the block. I came back in, locked the door, and walked straight past the kitchen piled high with dishes to lie down on the couch. It was the first time I'd sat down in twelve hours, and I had no intention of getting back up. I put my feet up and unbuttoned my pants, let the music play, and took in the room. The stacked Solo cups, the licked-clean plates, the sweaty wine bucket, the vases filled with flowers, the chairs pushed back from the table—irrefutable evidence that I am not just one person. In fact, I'm surrounded. I'm happy, I'm full, I'm still buzzing, and I'm definitely not doing those dishes tonight.

A proper "after" photo

The Easiest, Laziest, Most Brainless Party Snack That Still Manages to Impress

Makes about 3 cups

2 pints briny green olives, such as Castelvetrano and/or Lucques

1 cup raw almonds

1 lemon

1 orange

2 teaspoons aniseed

1 teaspoon Aleppo or other mildly spicy red chile flakes

Kosher salt; freshly ground black pepper

Extra-virgin olive oil, for drizzling

Drain the olives and put them in a smallish skillet, along with the almonds. Working over the skillet, use a vegetable peeler to remove the zest from the lemon and orange, avoiding the pith, allowing them to drop from the peeler right into the pan. Add the aniseed and Aleppo and season generously with salt and black pepper. Pour in enough olive oil to generously coat the olives and almonds, and then a few tablespoons more. Shake the skillet to roll everything in the oil.

Place the skillet over medium-low heat and cook, stirring occasionally, until the almonds and spices are lightly toasted and the citrus zests are shriveled and lightly browned, about 30 minutes.

Serve warm, with little bowls nearby for collecting the pits.

Celery-Fennel Salad with Anchovy Pesto Dressing

12 servings

2 medium fennel bulbs

6 to 8 medium celery stalks (6 ounces), thicker stalks peeled

3 large anchovy fillets in oil, drained

1 garlic clove, peeled but whole

½ cup toasted hazelnuts, divided

Kosher salt; freshly ground black pepper

3 tablespoons extra-virgin olive oil

½ teaspoon Aleppo pepper

½ teaspoon Urfa biber

1 tablespoon distilled white vinegar

1 tablespoon sherry vinegar

Flaky salt, for serving

Set aside a handful of fennel fronds and any pale celery leaves. Thinly slice the celery on a diagonal and transfer to a bowl of cold water. Cut the stems off the fennel bulbs, then cut each in half through the root. Thinly slice the fennel crosswise and add to the bowl with the celery. You should have about 8 cups sliced vegetables. Soak for about 15 minutes to make them extra crisp, then drain and blot dry.

> **Get ahead:** Wrap the prepped veggies in a clean kitchen towel, place in a vegetable bag, and refrigerate in the crisper drawer for up to 3 days.

Mince reserved fennel fronds and celery leaves. Set aside.

In a mortar and pestle, pound the anchovies, garlic, and ¼ cup hazelnuts to a paste. Season with salt and black pepper. Stir in the olive oil, Aleppo, and Urfa biber.

Roughly chop the remaining ¼ cup hazelnuts for topping the salad.

Place the celery and fennel in a large salad bowl. Stir both vinegars into the anchovy mixture; taste and adjust seasoning as needed. Add the vinaigrette to the sliced vegetables and toss thoroughly, until the dressing is evenly distributed and the vegetables are starting to release some liquid.

Serve topped with the chopped hazelnuts and a few pinches of flaky salt.

Aioli on Everything
Makes 2 cups

½ teaspoon black peppercorns

½ teaspoon coriander seeds

½ teaspoon cumin seeds

½ teaspoon fennel seeds

½ teaspoon mustard seeds

1½ cups vegetable oil

¼ cup extra-virgin olive oil

2 large egg yolks

2 tablespoons fresh lemon juice

2 garlic cloves, peeled but whole

Kosher salt

½ teaspoon dried mint

½ teaspoon Aleppo pepper

Pinch of sugar

Distilled white vinegar, white wine vinegar, or rice vinegar, for seasoning

Toast the black peppercorns and coriander, cumin, fennel, and mustard seeds in a small skillet over medium heat, shaking the pan frequently, until things start smelling good and some of the mustard seeds turn gray and pop, about 2 minutes. Transfer to a mortar and pestle and let cool, tossing occasionally. When cool, pound until finely ground. (Use a spice grinder if you'd rather!)

In a measuring cup or other vessel with a pouring spout, combine the vegetable oil and olive oil. In a medium bowl, whisk together the egg yolks, lemon juice, and 1 tablespoon cold water. Finely grate the garlic into the bowl and season with a big pinch of salt. Whisking constantly (but not exhaustively quickly), slowly drizzle in the oil mixture until you notice the egg mixture thicken and become opaque, like a small dollop of lemon yogurt. You have an emulsion. Take a break from whisking whenever you want from this point forward.

Continue adding oil and whisking until the aioli mixture is thickened and all of the oil has been incorporated. If the aioli becomes very thick or you notice that the oil floats on the surface and resists being absorbed, whisk in a tablespoon or two of water and carry on.

Add the mint and Aleppo and whisk to combine. Add the toasted spice mixture, ¾ teaspoon at a time, tasting as you go and adding salt as desired, until you're happy with the spice level. (You may not need all of it, but it's completely subjective. If making ahead, the spices will continue to open up and intensify, so err on underseasoning slightly in that case. You can always bump it up later.) Adjust the balance with a little sugar and a dash of vinegar.

Get ahead: Aioli can be made up to 5 days in advance. Cover and refrigerate. Whisk to loosen before serving.

Porchetta-Style Smoky Lamb Shoulder
Serves 12, with leftovers

1 tablespoon fennel seeds

2 teaspoons cumin seeds

1 tablespoon black peppercorns

1 teaspoon Aleppo pepper

2 teaspoons sweet paprika

1 boneless lamb shoulder (5 to 6 pounds), unrolled

2 tablespoons Diamond Crystal kosher salt or 4 teaspoons Morton

Flaky salt, for serving

In a small skillet, combine the fennel and cumin seeds and peppercorns. Set over medium heat and toast the spices, shaking the pan often to keep them moving, until lightly toasted and fragrant, about 4 minutes. Transfer to a mortar and add the Aleppo and paprika. Stir to combine; let the spices cool, tossing occasionally. Use a pestle to crush the spices until medium-ground.

Season the lamb on both sides with the kosher salt, then with the spice mixture, distributing evenly. Roll up the shoulder and tie it with butcher's twine, spacing the loops about 2 inches apart. Cover and chill for at least 24 hours and up to 3 days.

Preheat the oven to 225°F.

Place the lamb in a roasting pan or baking dish, cover loosely with foil, and cook until the internal temperature hits 200°F and stays about constant for an hour, 5 to 6 hours.

Remove the lamb from the oven and let cool in its juices, turning occasionally. At this point you can chill it, with its cooking liquid, for up to 2 days, or move ahead with the browning step.

Heat a grill for medium direct heat. Remove the lamb from the cooking liquid; strain the jus into a saucepan and cook over indirect heat until simmering. Meanwhile, grill the lamb, turning every few minutes, until browned and crisp all over and almost hot in the center, about 15 minutes on the grill. (Alternatively, preheat the oven to 400°F and roast the lamb on a rimmed baking sheet, turning every 5 minutes, until you reach the same end point.)

Let the lamb rest until cool enough to handle, then cut it into thin slices and arrange on a platter or in a large shallow bowl. Spoon some of the jus over and season with flaky salt. Serve remaining jus on the side so people can sauce their portions as desired.

Ross's Swole White Negroni
Makes enough for about thirty 3-ounce cocktails

1 bottle (750ml) Cocchi Americano

1 bottle (750ml) Lillet Blanc

1½ bottles (1.125L) London dry gin

20 dashes orange bitters

Ice (optional)

Lemon twists, for serving (optional)

In a large bowl or other container, combine the Cocchi, Lillet, and gin. Pour in 3 cups water and season with the bitters. Stir to combine. Transfer the Negroni base to a bottle or container with a 3½- to 4-quart capacity, then seal airtight, and freeze for up to 1 month. If the mixture is slushy, let sit at room temperature to temper.

Transfer the Negroni to a pitcher or leave in bottle. Serve the cocktails up in coupe glasses or over ice in rocks glasses, with a lemon twist, if desired.

Spicy Sesame Bean Sprouts
4 servings

12 ounces soybean sprouts

Drizzle of toasted sesame oil

Few dashes of soy sauce

Couple big pinches of gochugaru

Freshly ground pepper

Pinch of sugar

Few shakes of MSG

Kosher salt

Cook the sprouts in boiling salted water until they lose their raw flavor and are translucent and wilted, about 2 minutes. Drain and run under cold water to cool; shake off excess water.

Transfer the sprouts to a bowl and season to taste with sesame oil, soy sauce, gochugaru, pepper, sugar, and MSG. Add a pinch of salt if you think it needs it. This is great to the side of any grilled vegetables, fish, or meat.

Chile-Shallot Condiment
Makes 1 quart

3 red hot long peppers, such as Holland (2 ounces)

4 shallots (1 pound)

Kosher salt

¼ cup fresh lemon juice

3 tablespoons distilled white vinegar

Pinch of sugar

Thinly slice the peppers on a diagonal and transfer to a medium bowl. If you prefer a less spicy result, halve the peppers lengthwise, cut away the ribs, and scrape out the seeds first.

Thinly slice the shallots into thin rings and add to the bowl with the peppers. Season generously with salt and toss to distribute the salt and separate the shallot slices into individual rings. Add the lemon juice and vinegar and season with a 4-finger pinch of sugar. Toss again. The condiment is best if it sits at room temperature for a couple of hours before serving. It can also be covered and refrigerated for up to 3 days.

Special Thanks to These People

Eyes-closed crew photo, because I kept closing my eyes in photos

My readers, for giving my work a place to land

Michael, my therapist
Leslie Robarge, a saint among mortals
Omega, beloved collaborator and conspirer

Vanessa H., Fran, Roddy, Joey, Ross, Anne, Pat, Holli, Pony, Kelsey, Andrew, Kenny, Alivia, Amelia, Remy, Susie, Sam, Courtney, Andy, Emily, Rachel, Rory, Natalie, Jocelyn, Aunt Christina, Uncle Carlo, Aunt Susan, and Bob Pasta: I love you.

Sweet B., for communication, attention, and semi-regular teleportation

Alex Beggs, my very important top editor
Zan Goodman, endlessly brilliant, inspiring, and inspired designer
Cybelle Tondu, for her limitless expertise and care
Lucia Bell-Epstein, for fully and completely seeing it

Nathan Uren, Xander Rapparport, Layton Davis, Lola Katan, and Noa Rosenberg, for making our shoot so special

Francis Lam, my thoughtful editor at Clarkson Potter
Katherine Cowles, my fantastic agent

Jenna Bouma, for her art
Pamela Adlon, my starfishing queen

Frankie and Coppa, for our treasured family
Nina Lalli, my forever favorite person

And most of all: Leo and Cosmo, my excellent children. Being your parent gives me unquantifiable amounts of purpose, pride, and happiness.

All the Recipes, Part by Part

Recipe Index

D

E

F

G

All the events in this book took place in reality and were transformed by my consciousness, my fallible memory, and the passage of time. Some settings have been reimagined to protect the privacy of others. Anyone present during certain events will surely have their own version of what transpired. Misremembered or not, everything here matches my mind's eye. —C. L.

Clarkson Potter/Publishers
An imprint of the Crown Publishing Group
A division of Penguin Random House LLC
1745 Broadway
New York, NY 10019
clarksonpotter.com
penguinrandomhouse.com

Library of Congress Cataloging-in-Publication Data has been applied for.

ISBN 978-0-593-80062-1
Ebook ISBN 978-0-593-80063-8

Editor: Francis Lam | Editorial assistant: Darian Keels
Art direction and design: Zan Goodman, Zan Inc.
Production editor: Joyce Wong
Production: Philip Leung
Compositors: Merri Ann Morrell and Zoe Tokushige
Food stylist: Cybelle Tondu | Food stylist assistant: Nathan Uren
Prop stylist: Nina Lalli | Prop stylist assistant: Lola Katan
Photo assistants: Xander Rapparport and Layton Miles Davis | Photo retoucher: Vitreous Post
Location manager: Leo Music | Nail artist: Colette Gallant
Copy editor: Kate Slate | Proofreaders: Alisa Garrison, Miriam Garron, Erica Rose, and Bridget Sweet
Indexer: Elizabeth Parson
Marketer: Stephanie Davis | Publicist: Jina Stanfill

Manufactured in China

10 9 8 7 6 5 4 3 2 1

First Edition

The authorized representative in the EU for product safety and compliance is Penguin Random House Ireland, Morrison Chambers, 32 Nassau Street, Dublin D02 YH68, Ireland, https://eu-contact.penguin.ie.

SCRAP
COCONUT BASE
STACY'S PITA
MASALA
PORK CHOP
KIMCHI
STOCK 2/6
PISTACHIO
butter
SCALLIONS
DRIED
ALEPPO
ALMONDS
NEGRONI
honey
salsa
Chia
HZLNUT
SOUR CREAM
Gochujang
RAMP PESTO
WATERMELON SALAD
CARROTS
NEGRONI
JASMINE
CASTELVETRANO
SUSHI
SPROUTS
BLK. PEPCORNS
DATES
OCTOPUS DUMPLING
3 LARGE EGGS
TUNA

FRIED SHALLOT
tapioca 5/27
PANKO
edamame
MUSHROOM
buckwheat tea
sauce
BOLOGNESE 3/26
TOFU
HERB MASH
tuna salad
STOCK 2/6
Rice
CHICKPEAS v.2
FROZ. BLOOBS
LAMB DUMPL'GS
NDALOO
PASTA W/CHICKPEAS
BOB'S PEARL BARLEY
SPICY
honey nut
Rice
LAMB JUICE
SUSHI RICE
HOJI-
tuna SALAD
CORNICHOS
OR EVOO
MARGIE

SCRAP
COCONUT BASE
STACY'S PITA
MASALA
PORK CHOP
mann's mayo
KIMCHI
STOCK 2/6
PISTACHIO
butter
SCALLIONS
DRIED
ALEPPO
ALMONDS
NEGRONI
salsa
chia
HZLNUT
SOUR CREAM
gochujang
RAMP PESTO
WATERMELON SALAD
CARROTS
NEGRONI
JASMINE
CASTELVETRANO
SUSHI
SPROUTS
BLK. PEPCORNS
DATES
OCTOPUS DUMPLING
3 LARGE EGGS
TUNA
COCONUT BASE

FRIED SHALLOT
tapioca 5/27
PANKO
edamame
buckwheat tea
sauce
BOLOGNESE 3/26
TOFU
HERB MASH
tuna salad
STOCK 2/6
Rice
CHICKPEAS v.2
FROZ. BLOOBS
LAMB DUMPL'GS
NDALOO
PASTA W/CHICKPEAS
BOB'S PEARL BARLEY
SPICY
honey nut ♡
Rice
LAMB JUICE
SUSHI RICE
tuna SALAD
CORNICHOS
evoo
MARGIE